Divine Communication

Divine Communication

Word and Sacrament in Biblical, Historical, and Contemporary Perspective

HANS SCHWARZ

Fortress Press Philadelphia

Library of Congress Cataloging in Publication Data

Schwarz, Hans, 1939–
Divine communication.

Bibliography: p.
Includes indexes.
1. Word of God (Theology). 2. Baptism. 3. Lord's Supper. I. Title.
BT180.W67S38 1985 231.7'4 84-48732
ISBN 0-8006-1846-7

1416J84 Printed in the United States of America 1-1846

Contents

Preface

Within the last decade committees, commissions, and boards have been busy in virtually every larger denomination revising existing worship materials or issuing new ones. One major reason for this renewed interest in worship is the feeling that worship cannot be oblivious to the changing times, moods, and local idiom. Another equally important reason is the growing ecumenical awareness. So many dialogues on various levels have been going on between denominations that they invariably touch the worship life of the participating Christian communities. Thus, for example, materials from the Southern Hymnody appear in the *Lutheran Book of Worship* and Luther's battle hymn of the Reformation, "A Mighty Fortress Is Our God," is sung in Roman Catholic services.

This growing perception of the unity we share is best reflected in that which gives rise to Christian worship: God's self-communication in word and sacrament. Since denominational differences are not overcome by historical neglect but only glossed over, I would like to attempt to present a biblical, historical, and systematic outline of the major issues regarding word and sacrament. Quite frequently a historical approach will shed new light on the emergence of denominational differences and indicate avenues for overcoming them. In some ways this book will supplement my earlier publication, *The Christian Church*, in which word and sacraments received only passing attention. Though the inquisitive reader will not find here an all-encompassing description and analysis of word and sacrament, it is hoped that at least some major emphases are visible for a joint witness to God's self-communication.

My thanks go to Jon Temme and Craig Nessan for improvements in style and content and for completion of the bibliography, to Barbara Berger and Barbara Fischer for typing of the various drafts with speed and accuracy, and once again to Ron Grissom for proofreading the galleys and compiling the indexes. I would like to dedicate this book to my wife who cheerfully shares the joys and burdens of being married to a resident theologian.

Regensburg, West Germany HANS SCHWARZ

Abbreviations

ANF	Ante-Nicene Fathers: Translations of the Writings of the Fathers down to A.D. 325. Edited by Alexander Roberts and James Donaldson. 10 vols. New York: Christian Literature Co., 1886–97. Reprint: Wm. B. Eerdmans
ACW	Ancient Christian Writers. Paramus, N.J.: Paulist/Newman Press
BC	*The Book of Concord: The Confessions of the Evangelical Lutheran Church.* Trans. and ed. Theodore G. Tappert. Philadelphia: Fortress Press, 1959
CA	Confessio Augustana (Augsburg Confession)
CR	*Corpus Reformatorum.* Berlin and Leipzig, 1834–
FC	The Fathers of the Church. Washington, D.C.: Catholic University Press of America
LBW	*Lutheran Book of Worship.* Minneapolis: Augsburg; Philadelphia: Fortress Press
LW	*Luther's Works.* Philadelphia: Fortress Press; St. Louis: Concordia, 1955–
NPNF	Nicene and Post-Nicene Library of the Fathers. First series: Edited by Philip Schaff; 14 vols.; New York: Christian Literature Co., 1886–90; Reprint: Wm. B. Eerdmans. Second series: Edited by Philip Schaff and Henry Wace; 14 vols.; New York: Christian Literature Co., 1891–99; Reprint: Wm. B. Eerdmans
RE^3	*Realenzyklopädie für protestantische Theologie und Kirche.* Edited by A. Hauch. 3d ed. Leipzig, 1896–1913

RGG[3]	*Die Religion in Geschichte und Gegenwart.* Edited by K. Galling. 5 vols. 3d ed. Tübingen, 1957–65
TRE	*Theologische Realenzyklopädie.* Berlin and New York: Walter de Gruyter, 1977–
TDNT	*Theological Dictionary of the New Testament.* 9 vols. Grand Rapids: Wm. B. Eerdmans, 1964–73
WA	*D. Martin Luthers Werke.* Kritische Gesamtausgabe. Weimar, 1883–
WA DB	*D. Martin Luthers Werke.* Deutsche Bibel. Weimar, 1906–61

Introduction

> In many and various ways God spoke of old to our fathers by the prophets; but in these last days he has spoken to us by a Son.
>
> (Heb. 1:1–2)

How does God speak to us today? Through a vision, a dream, in our heart, through friends, or unusual events? When we reflect upon the God-disclosive Judeo-Christian history, we find all of these different means of communication confirmed. We hear, for example, that Joseph is instructed in a dream to flee with the holy family to Egypt, we read of Isaiah's vision in the temple, and we hear of Balaam's ass. These are just a few of the God-disclosive events encountered in Scripture. But how can we distinguish the divine communication from mere imagination or from accidental historical constellations? More pointedly, how do I know that God speaks to me and that it is not just my selfish ego that construes a "divine" rationale for its action?

While it is impossible to prevent selfish misuse of God's self-communication, the Judeo-Christian tradition developed at least one criterion to discern between pious self-justification and God's directing and life-transforming word: the awareness of a gracious and steadfast God. We notice this criterion as especially operative in Jesus, who cut through layers of words designed to assure correct appropriation of God's will and asked bluntly: What is the actual intention of God's word? or, What is the direction of *the* word among all of these words? Reviewing the God-disclosive history of the Judeo-Christian tradition we cannot but notice a continuum of one word among all other words, a continuum of grace in the midst of judgment, a word which admonishes to direct, which tears down to build up, and which scolds to assure. This continuum of grace interspersed with the reminder of obedience to God's will is *the* word among all other words. This word also has its visual side in the events of history when they are subjectively and existentially interpreted as God speaking to us, and above all in the so-called visible word, God's sacramental communication of his grace.

Small wonder that *the* word and the sacraments are crucial for the Christian to discern and appropriate God's self-communication.[1] But at the same time they cause a lot of questions: How is it possible that God should be communicated through words and objects? Should we understand this as crudely magical in a manipulative sense as a way of getting hold of God? Is it a symbolic, spiritual expression of something beyond our comprehension? Or are we simply talking about sacred rituals that have largely lost their original mystic meaning?

Most religions employ means very similar to those in the Christian faith by which they claim to be in contact with God or the divine. These may be sacred writings, ritual meals, initiation rites, propitiatory sacrifices, or prescribed washings and anointings. We might wonder to what extent the Christian understanding of divine self-communication is simply shared with the rest of the religious milieu out of which the Christian faith originated.

The issue is further complicated since the means employed are intimately connected with the experiential side of humanity. The question then arises as to how causally these means can be empirically described. In other words, can we demonstrate that their "results" stem from God or do they simply arise from within the emotional sphere of the individual; and is there a way to ascertain that these "results" of divine self-communication are truly effective within the recipient? The judgment of Friedrich Nietzsche—that Christians should look much more redeemed if there should be any reality connected with the Christian faith—cannot be ignored. We dare not suppress these issues in our investigation, although we cannot approach them without carefully probing into the nature of the Christian sacraments. We must first acknowledge that word and sacraments are central to the Christian community.

Until recent times the Roman Catholic Church has been a

predominately sacramental institution intent on assuring its adherents that it administers the means of grace. In contrast, mainline Protestant churches have often been called the churches of the word, that is, God's disclosive word. When we mention word and sacraments as two distinct entities we certainly do not want to leave the impression that the sacraments are void of *the* word or of words. The interpretative word (e.g., words of institution) is a constitutive part of any sacrament. The phrase "word and sacrament," frequently used in theological discourse, should more precisely be understood as "preached word and sacrament." Yet when we talk about a theology of the word, we do not mean a theology of the preached word, but a theology of the word of God in its most inclusive sense, implying also a consideration of the word made flesh. Word in this sense is intimately tied to the God-disclosive history reflected in the biblical documents.

It may surprise some that the term "means of grace," comprising word and sacrament, is not a biblical one. While the term "word" (*logos* or *rhema*) is attested in the New Testament, the term "sacrament" is missing there. We learn in Luke-Acts of the Christian community in Jerusalem that "day by day, attending the temple together and breaking bread in their homes, they partook of food with glad and generous hearts" (Acts 2:46). This passage depicts a very early stage in the life of the Christian community. In addition to hearing the word of God in the temple they also had their own gatherings around word and sacrament. Thus we read in Acts 2:42: "And they devoted themselves to the apostles' teaching and fellowship, to the breaking of bread and the prayers." We see here that the life of these Christians revolved around the word (Scripture and catechetical instruction) and sacrament (eucharistic fellowship). The meaning and significance of word and sacrament, however, can only be understood properly if we consider them in the context of the Jewish community out of which the Christian church emerged, and in relationship to Jesus Christ, the founder of the Christian church.

NOTES

1. For comprehensive studies of this topic from a different perspective one may consult Bernard J. Cooke, *Ministry to Word and Sacraments. His-*

tory and Theology (Philadelphia: Fortress Press, 1976), and Robert W. Jenson, *Visible Words. The Interpretation and Practice of Christian Sacraments* (Philadelphia: Fortress Press, 1978). We must also note the results of bilateral denominational conversations such as *One Baptism for the Remission of Sins, Eucharist and Ministry,* and *Eucharist as Sacrifice,* resulting from the Lutheran–Roman Catholic dialogues in the U.S.

1

The Biblical Understanding of the Word of God

Though appropriated by human conceptuality, the word of God is not a word about God but a word from God and thereby a word through which God discloses himself to us. Since it enacts history, God's word is not separable from his actions. Jesus Christ is God's final word both in the sense of his ultimate self-disclosure and in bringing his history with us to completion through his redemptive word and work. The incarnation of God's word in Jesus Christ opens for us full access to God.

THE WORD AS A MEANS OF GOD'S SELF-DISCLOSURE

When we reflect on the word of God, the question emerges whether we mean a word about God or from God. In his incisive essay, "What Does It Mean to Speak of God?" (1925), Rudolf Bultmann attempted to clear the issue when he claimed: "If 'speaking of God' is understood as 'speaking about God,' then such speaking has no meaning whatever, for its subject, God, is lost in the very moment it takes place."[1] If God is the reality determining all else, speaking about God would actually be a contradiction in terms, since it would presuppose a standpoint external to that which is being talked about. Since there can be no standpoint external to God, it is not legitimate to speak about God in general statements of universal truth that presume to be valid without reference to the concrete, existential position of the speaker.

Karl Barth sensed something of this difficulty when he stated: "*As ministers we ought to speak of God. We are human, however, and so cannot speak of God. We ought therefore to recognize both* our obligation and our inability *and by that very recognition give God the glory.*"[2] But Bultmann does not give up the difficult task of proclaiming the word of God, and neither did Barth. Bultmann continues: "we can speak of him [God] only in so far as we are speaking of his Word spoken to us, of his act done to us. 'Of God we can only tell what he does to us,'" reiterating a statement by Wilhelm Herrmann.[3] Since we are on earth, we cannot speak of God in the true sense. But unless we want to recede into mystical silence, we must speak about God, although we know that any speech about God is necessarily inadequate.

We conclude from these considerations (that are informed by Søren Kierkegaard's insistance on the infinite qualitative difference between God and humanity) that any word about God cannot be a word that has humanity as its initiator. To be of any significance in "describing God," it must be a word that describes us as we understand ourselves addressed by God. Word about God means a reflection of God's word to us. Word about God cannot be a descriptive statement about God, but an approximation of how God acts with us. Paul Tillich captured this situation very well when he mentioned in volume 2 of his *Systematic Theology* "that everything religion has to say about God, including his qualities, actions, manifestations, has a symbolic character and that the meaning of 'God' is completely missed if one takes the symbolic language literally." Asking himself whether a nonsymbolic statement about God is possible, he concludes: "There is a point at which a nonsymbolic assertion about God must be made . . . , namely, the statement that everything we say about God is symbolic."[4] With this concession Tillich has recognized that any word about God has at best symbolic character. For Tillich, however, this does not mean these words are of no value.

Tillich distinguished between sign and symbol saying, "while the sign bears no necessary relation to that to which it points, the symbol participates in the reality of that for which it stands."[5] A religious symbol not only points to the divine, but, if it is a true symbol, participates in the power of the divine. Reviewing the abundant literature concerning the God issue, however, one wonders whether the symbols advanced there actually disclosed much about God since there seems to be hardly any consensus about them. Wolfgang Trillhaas characterized the situation very aptly when he said:

> Each dogmatician, especially among the modern ones, decrees the attributes [of God] differently than another, so that one cannot refute the impression that this process is governed by a certain arbitrary speculation which is nourished by the richness of biblical and at the same time philosophical tradition.[6]

Friedrich Schleiermacher sensed this subjective and speculative tendency when he mentioned that after the age of scholasticism metaphysics was treated separately and apart from Christian doctrine in the philosophical discipline called natural theology. Yet he asserted that we should not forget that the representations of the divine attributes are of religious and not of philosophical origin. "All attributes which we ascribe to God are to be taken as denoting not something special in God, but only something special in the manner in which the feeling of absolute dependence is to be related to Him."[7] In other words, the adjectives we attribute to God are neither descriptive of him nor do they originate from human fantasy. They are an attempt to express how we experience God's relationship to us. To talk about God and his likeness is different from speaking in a raised voice about us. If these concepts truly express how we experience God's relationship to us, they indeed disclose some modality of God to us. Or, to use Tillich's terminology, they are true symbols and participate in the power of the divine to which they point.

It should become clear, however, that these concepts do not disclose God in his divine "essence," that is, apart from his self-disclosure. Luther stated this restriction very appropriately when he said:

> It is therefore insane to argue about God and the divine nature without the Word or any covering. . . . Whoever desires to be saved and to be safe when he deals with such great matters, let him simply hold on to the form, the signs, and the coverings of the Godhead, such as His Word and His works. For in His Word and in His work He shows Himself to us.[8]

On another occasion he also warned:

> Through their speculations some ascend into heaven and speculate about God the creator, etc. Do not get mixed up with this God. Whoever wishes to be saved should move away from God in his majesty, for He and the human creature are enemies. Rather grasp that God whom David also grasps. He is the God who is clothed in his promises. . . . Such a God one must have. . . . We know no other God than the one who is clothed in his promises. If he would talk to me in his majesty I would run away like the Jews did. But when he is clothed in the voice of man and accommodated himself to our capacity to understand, I can approach him.[9]

It would be interesting to speculate about the omnipotence or the aseity of God. Yet the only direction we can get in our desire to talk theologically about God is the God-disclosive history that culminated in Jesus Christ. This does not mean that philosophical concepts concerning God's being are without validity. The reflection on God's self-disclosure as recorded in the Bible is not written in original "Bible language." It shows on almost every page that its conceptuality is borrowed from many different sources. But all conceptual tools must be judged, transformed, or verified by the degree to which they support the coming into language of the one who disclosed himself in this history. Since the whole disclosive history culminated in God's final self-disclosure in Jesus Christ, we might also say that the meaning and truth attributed to all such (philosophical and religious) experiences and concepts must be determined with the reference to Jesus Christ.

Wolfhart Pannenberg made a significant observation in his "Dogmatic Theses on the Doctrine of Revelation" when he stated in the first thesis: "The self-revelation of God in the biblical witnesses is not of a direct type in the sense of a theophany, but is indirect and brought about by means of the historical acts of God."[10] Word of God is not a direct propositional statement, saying that God is this and that way or that God demands this or that. God's word does not provide a self-descriptive analysis of God, but it is a word that will not return empty. It refers us to what God is doing and to what we experience as his doings. This does not imply a totally subjective and existential understanding of God's word. Pannenberg states that God's self-disclosive history came to its climax in Jesus of Nazareth "insofar as the end of all events is anticipated in his fate."[11] God in Christ Jesus becomes the interpretative tool for all our present encounters with God's word.

We are reminded here of Luther's Reformation principle that "whatever communicated Christ is true and acceptable." Luther said in his picturesque way that "whatever does not teach Christ is certainly not apostolic even though St. Peter or St. Paul teach it. Again whatever preaches Christ is apostolic even though Judas, Annas, Pilate, or Herod might say it."[12] Any claim to represent the word of God must therefore be judged by comparing Jesus Christ with his ultimate Word. The finality of Jesus as God's disclosive or verbal history is again indicated in the statement: "In many and various ways God spoke of old to our fathers by the prophets; but in these last days he has spoken to us by a Son. . . . He reflects the glory of God and bears the very stamp of his nature" (Heb. 1:1–3). In Jesus' words and actions God himself is reflected. Yet, in attempting to describe the Word of God, we cannot confine ourselves to Jesus since Jesus himself cannot be properly understood without the Jewish background out of which he emerged. Talking about the word of God, we must first investigate its biblical origin and usage.

THE HISTORY-MAKING POWER OF GOD'S WORD

When we investigate the biblical writings, we encounter three terms that are especially important to elucidating the meaning of the word of God: the Hebrew *dabar*, and the Greek *logos* and *rhema*. In the Septuagint the Hebrew *dabar* is usually translated as *logos* or *rhema*. In Hellenism *logos* obtains great significance as the world reason, the world law; and the *logos spermatikos*, the active principle in the world. Some of this usage may not be unrelated to the Hebrew understanding of the word since the founder of the Stoa, Zeno of Citium, was of Semitic (Phoenician) origin and he especially emphasized the significance of the *logos*.

The term *dabar* gains special theological prominence in the Old Testament prophecy. A prophet does not speak on his own; but as we hear of David, "The Spirit of the Lord speaks by me, his word is upon my tongue" (2 Sam. 23:2). The Spirit of God speaks through a person, using him or her as a medium for his self-disclosure. The reception of God's word through a prophet is a Spirit-worked event. Yet in the Old Testament the connection between *pneuma* (Spirit) and word is not as evident as it is in the New Testament. The spiritual dimension is contained in every assertion concerning God's self-disclosure, and a prophet such as Hosea calls himself a "man of the spirit" (Hosea 9:7).

Initially revelation mainly occurred through signs in which the word was expressed, such as the oracles of Balaam (Num. 24:2–9, 15–24). Eventually the word itself was considered the medium of God's self-disclosure. In the writings of the Old Testament prophets we then find the frequent opening: "The word of the Lord that came to . . ." (Hosea 1:1, Micah 1:1). The word of God is present from the beginning of a prophetic existence. For instance, Isaiah introduces his speech with "the word which Isaiah the son of Amoz saw concerning Judah and Jerusalem" (Isa. 2:1). We also notice a close connection between word and Torah. In Isa. 1:10 we encounter the prophet's appeal: "Hear the word [*dabar*] of the Lord, you rulers of Sodom! Give ear to the teaching [*Torah*] of our God, you people of Gomorrah!" In Jeremiah we observe that the law belongs to the priest, while the word is associated with the prophet (Jer. 18:18). For Jeremiah the law is already present in written form, and he remarks that "the false pen of the scribes has made it into a lie" (Jer. 8:8). The main concern of the prophet, however, is not with the Torah, but with the word. He knows he has been set apart as a prophet before he was born, and he is sure that the Lord put his words into the prophet's mouth (Jer. 1:5, 9).

Jeremiah also distinguished between prophecy and the prophet who proclaims God's word when he related: "Let the prophet who has a dream tell the dream, but let him who has my word speak my word faithfully. What has the straw in common with wheat? says the Lord" (Jer. 23:28). He also stated a difference between normal prophecy, in which truth can be disclosed, and the proclamation of God's word. The word of God is an irresistible force, like fire in which the chaff is consumed or like a hammer which breaks the rock

(Jer. 23:29). Jeremiah wrestles with the word of God in terms of his own destiny as a prophet, and he realizes that the word of God transcends his personal limitations. This has been forcefully emphasized by Deutero-Isaiah. He perceives God's word as a historical force, and God's self-disclosure is seen as worked out in the development of things. "The grass withers, the flower fades; but the word of our God will stand for ever" (Isa. 40:8). The word of God is a powerful agent that will bring results with the same certainty as do the forces of nature (Isa. 55:10–11). The word of God is a divine power that creatively accomplishes its work on earth. It executes God's will and does what it is set out to do.

The word is the medium of God's self-disclosure so that the self-disclosure does not occur without the word, as, for instance, in a theophany. The word discloses God and his will. This is true for the prophetic word and for the word of law. The law is God's word and underlies the divine covenant (Exod. 24:7–8; 34:27–28). Again this Word is a forceful agent. God pledges himself to his people to sustain and guide them. But if they do not live up to the covenant, this means ruin for them. Thus God's word encounters the Israelites in a twofold way: as promise and threat. It is significant that the divine word or God's commandment is not beyond the people's grasp. It is neither spatially nor geographically removed from them. In Deuteronomy we read that "the word is very near you; it is in your mouth and in your heart, so that you can do it" (Deut. 30:14). God's commanding word is not uttered in a distant land or in an esoteric language. It is accessible to everyone so that there is no excuse for not listening to it.

The word of God is not simply an instrument to certain things, but *it carries with it the power to bless or to condemn.* If people follow it, God will bless them and their land. But if they turn away, they will perish and the land they possess will be taken away from them (Deut. 30:16–18). The Israelites are then admonished: "I have set before you life and death, blessing and curse; therefore choose life, that you and your descendants may live, loving the Lord your God, obeying his voice, and cleaving to him; for that means life to you and length of days" (Deut. 30:19–20). God's word encounters us as accusing and condemning or as promising and freeing. Yet in both cases it is conceived of as an active and powerful word. It affects the life of the people and communicates God's will. This will is not confined to the sphere of the individual or of nations, but it also affects nature.

God's word is the agent through which the world is created and sustained. Genesis 1 prominently features the ease with which everything is created through God's word. "God said . . . and there was" is the continuous assertion in the priestly creation story. The emphasis on the creative word of God is continued in the Old Testament by Deutero-Isaiah when he asserts that God calls everything by its name, that is, he has the power over all things (Isa. 40:26), and that he tells the deep to dry up, that is, he brings forth the dry land (Isa. 44:27). God's word is creative of history and nature. He directs the forces of nature to the ends he has decreed, and he guides history according to his will. For instance, he says of Cyrus, " 'He is my shepherd, and he shall fulfil all my purpose'; saying of Jerusalem, 'She shall be built'; and of the temple, 'Your foundation shall be laid' " (Isa. 44:28). Similarly, we hear in some of the psalms how God creates and directs the world and its history with his word: "He sends forth his command to the earth; his word runs swiftly" and "He declares his word to Jacob, his statutes and ordinances to Israel" (Ps. 147:15, 19). God's word, being active in human history and nature, creates, directs, and sustains the world. It also pronounces judgment and announces forgiveness. This understanding of God's word is continued in the New Testament.

JESUS CHRIST AS GOD'S FINAL WORD

"The emphasis which the whole of the New Testament places on hearing . . . presupposes a preceding speaking."[13] Jesus occupies a prominent place in relation to the word because of his proclamation and his demand that the people listen to him. Work and word of Jesus do not function independently of each other, but his word is a working and active word. It is an integral part of his mission. For instance, in the story of the healing of the paralytic, he first announces to the man that his sins are forgiven. Only then did Jesus heal him, to demonstrate that "the Son of man has authority on earth to forgive sins" (Mark 2:10). This sequence is indicative of the flow of Jesus' activity. He never does something without using it as an illustration of his proclamation.

Occasionally in the New Testament people call Jesus a prophet. But can he justifiably be called a prophet? We do not hear that he himself refers to the word of God or to a word that was given to him which he had to reveal. Neither at his baptism nor in the story of the transfiguration do we hear that God's word comes to Jesus, as we could assume if there existed an affinity to the Old Testament prophets. It would only have been natural that someone who did as much preaching and teaching as Jesus would also have a special word from God. Yet he is not commissioned at baptism to a specific ministry of the word, but he is acclaimed as God's Son. Gerhard Kittel rightly concludes that "there can be only one reason why the idea of a detailed word of God imparted to Jesus Himself has not found its way into the record. This is that such an idea was felt to be inappropriate and inadequate to describe the relationship of Jesus with God."[14]

Jesus confesses, according to Matthew: "All things have been delivered to me by my Father; . . . and no one knows the Father except the Son and any one to whom the Son chooses to reveal him" (Matt. 11:27). This shows a much more intimate relationship between Jesus and God than could be expected to exist between God and a prophet. Jesus does not just bring a word from God, but he brings the whole word and the total God. The closeness between God and Jesus is also expressed in that there is no discernible distinction in the New Testament between the terms "the word of God," "the word of the Lord," and "the word." They are simply used alongside each other, with the "word of God" being used thirty times, the "word of the Lord" eight times, and "the word" forty times. This nondistinction between the word of God and the word of the Lord again seems to have its origin in Jesus. Ernst Fuchs has convincingly pointed out that Jesus emphasized in his own proclamation the will of God in such a way as only someone could do who stood in God's place.[15] For instance, in his parables Jesus did not simply tell his audience how God acts, but he told them that God acts the way he himself acts. We see this especially in the parable of the Lost Sheep (Luke 15:3–7). When the Pharisees and scribes remarked, "This man receives sinners and eats with them" (Luke 15:2), Jesus told them in parables of God's concern for the lost and the sinful, implying that God acts like Jesus. The identification of Jesus and God can also be seen in Jesus' use of the term *ego eimi* ("I am") which he uses similar to the Old Testament theophany formula and in his use of the term *abba*.[16]

The identification of Jesus with the word and with God was continued in the first Christian community. There was an awareness that proclaiming what had taken place in the person of Jesus meant proclaiming the word and that reception of the word implied faith in Jesus. Paul states that he

> became a minister according to the divine office which was given to me for you, to make the word of God fully known, the mystery hidden for ages and generations but now made manifest to the saints. To them God chose to make known how great among the Gentiles are the riches of the glory of this mystery, which is Christ in you, the hope of glory.
> (Col. 1:25–27)

We are not provided with a theory of the word, but are told that the word which is the center of Paul's ministry arises from the event of Jesus. Similarly, we hear that it is essential for the Twelve to preach the word of God and, what is synonymous, to devote themselves to prayer and to "the ministry of the word" (Acts 6:2, 4). When the ranks of the Twelve were replenished, it was only natural that a candidate should be "one of the men who have accompanied us during all the time that the Lord Jesus went in and out among us, beginning from the baptism of John until the day when he was taken from us—one of these men must become with us a witness to his resurrection" (Acts 1:21–22). In serving the word of God, the Twelve were eyewitnesses of Jesus, the incarnation of God's word.

It should also be noted at this point that the original New Testament designation for the gospel tradition was *logos* or *logos theou* and not *euangelion*, which denoted the missionary appeal.[17] These terms correspond with the names then current in Judaism for Holy Scripture. The life and words of Jesus were understood in analogy to the Old Testament writings as the word of God for the new covenant community. The identification of Jesus with the *logos* is most prominent in the Gospel of John. Especially in the prologue do we find emphasis on the historical and spatiotemporal concreteness of the *logos*. The word was not just something to be heard with the ear. It was also not just mediated through the speaking and teaching of Jesus. Jesus Christ was the word in person. There is no speculation about the *logos* in terms of personification or in identifying it with the Torah. All considerations of the *logos* focus on the statement that the *logos* became incarnate in the historical person of Jesus, or, to say it more precisely, that the historical figure of Jesus was the *logos* through whom God had spoken in the Old Testament. God's word had not only been conveyed by certain people in the Old Testament, now he spoke personally in Jesus of Nazareth. Consequently, Jesus could claim of himself: "I do nothing on my own authority but speak thus as the Father taught me" (John 8:28).

The identification between God and Jesus is not restricted to the Johannine corpus. For instance, in Luke 10:16 we read in connection with the sending of the seventy: "He who hears you hears me, and he who rejects you rejects me, and he who rejects me rejects him who sent me." The identification with God is extended here even to the disciples. The word does not stop with Jesus but is continued in those whom Jesus sent. The continuity between sender (God), medium (Jesus), and proclamation (the disciples) is especially well expressed in the opening of the First Letter of John:

> That which was from the beginning, which we have heard, which we have seen with our eyes, which we have looked upon and touched with our hands, concerning the word of life—the life was made manifest, and we saw it, and testify to it, and proclaim to you the eternal life which was with the Father and was made manifest to us—that which we have seen and heard we proclaim also to you.
>
> (1 John 1:1–3)

The word of life made manifest is the content of the Christian proclamation and of God's word. Jesus is the bringer of life and of God's word. He who hears his word and believes in him who sent him "has eternal life; he does not come into judgment, but has passed from death to life" (John 5:24).

God's Word is not information about something, but communication with God's will, which is fundamentally the announcement of new life. But John leaves no doubt that not everyone will accept Jesus and the word. By rejecting Jesus and God's word, one rejects God as the source of life and chooses damnation and death. As we have seen in the Old Testament, the word of God is an active word in those who encounter and accept it. Though judgment is an intrinsic part of the encounter with God's word, John does not see the word as a judging word. The judgment is rather brought about by the people themselves. In the Synoptics, however, the notion of the judgment day at which the faithful will be separated from the faithless is so prevalent that we get the impression that the word of God is an active word bringing blessing or doom. The word does not leave anybody in a neutral corner, but necessitates a response which results either in acceptance and life or in rejection and death.

God's word is not confined to the strictly personal sphere. For instance, in the prologue of the Gospel of John, Jesus is identified with the word of the divine creator. He is first asserted as preexistent, being before the beginning of the world; and he is also introduced as the one through whom the whole world was created. The word of God is not impersonal as we might conclude from Genesis 1, but a personal word, incarnate as Jesus Christ. The Gospel of John does not start with speculation about the process of creation, but with the person of Jesus Christ in whom the creative word of God became flesh. Of course, the prologue bears analogies to Jewish thought (e.g., the role of wisdom as the divine agent of creation), which may have influenced the discourse. There also may be some parallels between the prologue and the Hellenistic speculations about the *logos*, as we can see now in the Gnostic literature of Nag Hammadi. Yet in John the main emphasis is on Jesus' relation to the Father which is expressed by identifying him with God's word. In sharp contrast to Gnostic or Hellenistic thought, there is no speculation in John about the word apart from its historical incarnation.

The inclusion of nature into the domain of the word is also displayed in the Synoptic material and in Paul. For instance, after Jesus calmed the sea, the people responded with awe and asked: "Who then is this, that even wind and sea obey him?" (Mark 4:41). The people rightly sensed the presence of the divine power when Jesus calmed the waves. The creative aspect of the word is also prominent in Paul's interpretation of the sacrament. Being drawn into the destiny of Jesus Christ, the word incarnate, the believers become new beings through baptism so that they "might walk in newness of life" (Rom. 6:4). Whoever is in Christ is a new creation, we hear Paul exclaim, emphasizing the creative benefits of Christ and the efficacy of his being God's word.

Unlike in the Old Testament, the emphasis on the blessings is not so much on their promissory aspect. Part of it has been realized through the coming of Christ. Those of you "who have heard the word of truth, the gospel of your salvation, and have believed in him, were sealed with the promised Holy Spirit, which is the guarantee of our inheritance until we acquire possession of it" (Eph. 1:13–14), Paul says. Something is already given to us through the coming of Christ. The situation has been changed from the hoping community of the Old Testament to the fulfillment in anticipation in the New Testament. The word of God has not returned empty; it has shown us a new avenue of life in Jesus Christ. Thus Christ becomes the center of hope and the focus of the Christian proclamation.

Since the Lutheran church has often been called the church of the word, it is not surprising that the man whose name it bears had much appreciation for the word. *Luther was convinced that Christ could be found nowhere except in the word*, that is, in the proclamation of the church. But the church cannot communicate Christ without reference to the biblical word. While this word is not mystical or internal, the word proclaimed by the church and centered in the Bible is not strictly external either, restricted to a language event. It is at the same time an internal word which touches our hearts and which we believe.

But without the external word, God does not give us his Spirit through whom we believe. The Spirit is not given in addition to the word. Luther assured us that the Spirit works in and through the word. With his insistence on the external word, Luther wanted to counteract any spiritualistic and overly enthusiastic inclinations that might emphasize the internal word to the near exclusion of its external aspect.

Since God addresses us throughout the history of his people, culminating in the life and destiny of Jesus Christ, there is no other way open to us to hear him but through the avenue of history. Luther asserted: "We must not, as the sectarians do, imagine that God comforts us immediately, without his Word. Comfort does not come to us without the Word, which the Holy Spirit effectively calls to mind and enkindles in our hearts, even though it has not been heard for ten years."[18] The word has divine power and convinces us that it is actually from God. The word does not need an external authorization, such as a teaching office, the Holy Spirit, or our intellect, to convince us of its truthfulness. The word itself, through the Spirit working in it, has convincing power where and when it chooses (cf. CA 5). The word is an independent entity that cannot be manipulated to yield desired results so that we could produce our own or someone else's conversion. Luther insisted that "God comes to me without any preparation or help on my part."[19]

Nevertheless, Luther insisted that we should preach, hear, and read the word. The reason for this is not that we can contribute anything to God's activity, but that God does not want to act apart from external means. He is active through the preached, heard, and read word. The means of grace, word and sacrament, are vital for God's communication of himself to us. While Luther emphasizes that God's word does everything, he implicitly acknowledges our cooperation by insisting on external mediation. Yet he maintains the primacy of God's action, since our doing does not necessitate God to act. He has decided to act before we ever hear his word or ask him for forgiveness.

God's word appropriates to us his self-disclosure in Jesus Christ. It is a word of promise, announcing to us participation in the new life in Christ and restoration as God's children. Since God does not confine his activity to the life of Christians or the Judeo-Christian history, the rest of creation also witnesses to God's creative, directive, and sustaining activity. This means that, in principle, his word and will are known in places in which his name is not adequately confessed. Of course, Luther is quick to admit that such knowledge of God and his word is not complete enough—due to our sinfulness and our wrong perception of his word—to ensure our salvation. For instance, Luther admits that "reason knows that there is a God. But who or what it is that is a true God, reason does not know."[20] Furthermore, God does not want to be sought after or found in the sublime things, but in the cradle and on the cross. Only the incarnation of God's word in Jesus Christ opens for us the full access to God. This access which is characterized as God's salvific action encounters us not just as promise and grace, it also contains the potential of threat. Consequently, God's word has often been described as law and gospel.

NOTES

1. Rudolf Bultmann, *Faith and Understanding*, ed. with an intro. by Robert W. Funk, trans. L. P. Smith (London: SCM Press, 1969), 53.

2. Karl Barth, "The Word of God and the Task of Ministry" (1922), in *The Word of God and the Word of Man*, trans. D. Horton (New York: Harper Torchbooks, 1957), 186. The German original reads "theologians" instead of "ministers." Cf. *Anfänge der dialektischen Theologie*, ed. by Jürgen Moltmann (Munich: Chr. Kaiser, 1966), 1:199.

3. Bultmann, *Faith and Understanding*, 63.

4. Paul Tillich, *Systematic Theology*, vol. 2: *Existence and the Christ* (Chicago and London: University of Chicago Press, 1957), 9.

5. Tillich, *Systematic Theology*, vol. 1: *Reason and Revelation. Being and God* (Chicago and London: University of Chicago Press, 1951), 239.

6. Wolfgang Trillhaas, *Dogmatik* (Berlin: Alfred Töpelmann, 1962), 121 (my trans.).

7. Friedrich Schleiermacher, *The Christian Faith*, ed. and trans. H. R. Mackintosh and J. S. Stewart (Edinburgh: T. & T. Clark, 1960), 194–95 (par. 50).

8. Martin Luther, Lectures on Genesis. Chapters 1–5, *LW* 1:13, in his comments on Gen. 1:2.

9. Martin Luther, Enarratio Psalmi LI (1538), *WA* 2, 329, 8–12 and 330, 1–7, in his exegesis of Ps. 51:3.

10. Wolfhart Pannenberg, "Dogmatic Theses on the Doctrine of Revelation," in *Revelation as History*, ed. W. Pannenberg, trans. D. Granskou (New York: Macmillan Co., 1968), 125.

11. Ibid., 139 (thesis 4).

12. Martin Luther, Vorrede auf die Epistel S. Jacobi und Jude (1546), *WA* DB 7, 384, 29–32.

13. Gerhard Kittel, "*lego*," in *TDNT* 4:100.

14. Ibid., 114.

15. Cf. Ernst Fuchs, *Studies of the Historical Jesus,* trans. A. Scobie (Naperville, Ill.: Alec R. Allenson, 1964), 154–55.

16. For the use of *ego eimi*, cf. Hans Schwarz, *On the Way to the Future* (rev. ed.; Minneapolis: Augsburg, 1979), 58ff.: for *abba*, cf. Joachim Jeremias, *New Testament Theology*, vol. 1: *The Proclamation of Jesus*, trans. J. Bowden (London: SCM Press, 1971).

17. Harald Riesenfeld, *The Gospel Tradition*, foreword W. D. Davies, trans. E. M. Rowley and R. A. Kraft (Philadelphia: Fortress Press, 1970), 20.

18. Martin Luther, The Beautiful Confitemini, *LW* 14:62, in his exegesis of Ps. 118:6.

19. Martin Luther, *WA* 12, 497, 2–3, in a sermon of 6 April 1523.

20. Martin Luther, Der Prophet Jona ausgelegt (1526), *WA* 19, 206, 32–33, in his exegesis of Jonah 1:5.

2

The Dynamics of God's Word

The same word of God meets us either as law or as gospel. The proper distinction between them is intrinsic to a full understanding of God's word. God's word does not vanish for the justified ones but they encounter it both as guidance to new life and as promise of being accepted. Since God's word asks for our response, prayer and liturgy are its proper verbal expression. In prayer we engage in a free but responsible dialogue with God, while liturgy is formalized dialogue in which some of God's actions are dramatized. The efficacy of God's word becomes especially noticeable in miracles. Though not proofs of God's activity, they remind us that he will bring his promises to conclusion.

THE JUDGING AND LIBERATING WORD (LAW AND GOSPEL)

One might wonder whether such a typically Lutheran term as "law and gospel" is adequate to characterize the dynamics of God's word. Yet we noticed in our brief biblical survey that God's word is indeed not just promise and grace; it can also be judging and condemning. Nevertheless, many systematic theologians avoid the term "law and gospel" altogether and talk instead about God's word. Even Luther confessed that terms are not important; the content only is decisive. Yet it facilitates the description of God's word when we classify its different receptions by distinct terms.

God's word as preserved by the Christian community and encountered in its teaching and proclamation, can basically assume one of three functions: If we rely on God's word, it is (1) a liberating and freeing word (*gospel*) and at the same time (2) a guiding and protecting word (*parenesis*). But if we assert ourselves and reject God's word, it will encounter us (3) as judgment and condemnation (*law*). Since the functional character of God's word is emphasized here, it should be evident that the functional distinction between the Mosaic law and the gospel is *not* synonymous with the difference between the Mosaic law and the gospel of Jesus Christ. This distinction is historically derived from Jesus' opposition to the pious legalism of his own people and from Paul's struggle with Judaizing tendencies in early Christianity. It is founded in a diametrically opposed function and perception of the same word of God.

The tendency to collapse the law into the gospel is a constant danger among Christians. Since God is loving and caring, there should be no threat connected with his word. As a consequence of this kind of reasoning, one often advocates love without a cost, and grace without consequences. Dietrich Bonhoeffer rightly protested against this "cheap grace" and in the same vein H. Richard Niebuhr warned against the attempt to preach a Christ without a cross, salvation without wrath, and a kingdom of our own desires. Especially from proponents of process thought the notion has been advocated that if God is to win the world, he must do so with love and not with force. For instance, Alfred North Whitehead praised Jesus as the Galilean vision of humility.

While God's grace rules supreme, we should not forget that a negative reaction to his grace does entail consequences. It is especially significant for our discussion that even Roman Catholic theologians insist that the distinction between law and gospel "is regarded as the distinctive feature of the Christian faith as contrasted not only with Judaism but also with all pagan religions, with philosophy, ethics, and the like."[1] The distinction between law and gospel is even more necessary because the impact of the law is also clearly felt outside the Christian realm.

The law has a twofold foundation. In its civil use it preserves the creation and guards it against destruction and chaos, while in its proper and theological use it serves to convict sinners of their transgressions against the Lord. This means that in its civil use it is concomitant with God's preserving activity and ought to be known by all of creation. The universal knowledge of the law has been advocated by the natural law tradition, especially prevalent among Roman Catholic theologians, but also among more conservative Protestants. Recently it has received renewed attention by ethologists who argue that there are basic norms of moral behavior that are common to all societies, human and nonhuman (cf. Wolfgang Wickler). Such common knowledge also seems to be advocated by the New Testament. For instance, Paul claims that

> When Gentiles who have not the law do by nature what the law requires, they are a law to themselves, even though they do not have the law. They show that what the law requires is written on their hearts, while their conscience also bears witness and their conflicting thoughts accuse or perhaps excuse them on that day when, according to my gospel, God judges the secrets of men by Christ Jesus.
>
> (Rom. 2:14–16)

Paul does not claim that the pagans know the law that was given to the Jews at Mt. Sinai, but they have something analogous to which they must be as responsive and responsible. The divine will is inscribed in their hearts from which they should know what to do.

Martin Luther inferred from Rom. 2:14 that if God had never given the written law through Moses, our human spirit would still know by nature that we should worship God and love our neighbor. In his disputes with the Antinomians, Luther argued that from the beginning of the world the Decalogue has been inscribed in the human mind.

> Therefore, there is one law which runs through all ages, is known to all men, is written in the hearts of all people, and leaves no one from beginning to end with an excuse, although for the Jews ceremonies were added and the other nations had their own laws, which were not binding upon the whole world, but only this one, which the Holy Spirit dictated unceasingly in the hearts of all.[2]

The natural law largely coincides with the law of Moses, but must be distinguished from the positive law of a country and also from the Jewish ceremonial law. Luther does not simply equate the Mosaic law with the natural law, since he is convinced that Moses interprets and clarifies the latter. Luther, therefore, states that the natural law "is clearly and well summarized at Mt. Sinai and in a better way than by the philosophers."[3]

For Luther and the New Testament tradition on which he based his reflections, the law inscribed in the hearts of all people is not just synonymous with its civil use or first use. It also fulfills a theological function since it expresses God's will and since all people are by nature religious. As Rom. 2:14–16 declares, God's eternal will is present in the human conscience. His will reminds us of our alienation from God and shows us that we do not live as we ought. Due to our alienation from God, this second, theological, and convicting use of the law is often obliterated even within the Judeo-Christian tradition. Nevertheless, all of us have the possibility of knowing God's will and thus we have no excuse for not living up to it.

When Paul says that "Law came in, to increase the trespass" (Rom. 5:20), we might at first wonder why God would give the law in order to evoke sin and to let it develop all its power. But would it make sense to assume that humanity was sinless until it was explicitly confronted with the law? Humanity clearly lived in sin long before the law was given on Mt. Sinai. As Jesus demonstrated in the Sermon on the Mount, however, often the transgressions against the law were not understood as such; and the realization of our sinful nature lay dormant. When God gave his law, sin was exposed and set free so that it could be perceived as what it actually was—revolt against God. In this sense, sin is increased and sharpened through the law. As Martin Luther experienced in his monastic life, the more conscientiously we attempt to fulfill God's will, the more we realize our shortcomings and discover our immense sinfulness. God's will, originally a sign of his love and care, has now been turned into a sign of despair and of God's wrath.

The law sharpens our conscience and shows us that we are in a hopeless predicament. Paul himself exclaims in despair: "For I know that nothing good dwells within me, that is, in my flesh. I can will what is right, but I cannot do it. For I do not do the good I want, but the evil I do not want is what I do" (Rom. 7:18–19). The preoccupation with the law leads to condemnation instead of salvation. Yet Luther also saw that without the preaching of the law we do not hear God's truth. The law does not just show us our shortcomings and condemn us, it also moves us to seek God's grace. This is also the opinion of John Calvin in his *Institutes of the Christian Religion* in which he shows this twofold movement of the law, toward judgment and toward grace, by adducing many quotations from Augustine. Grace confronts us in God's redemptive work in Christ.

In Rom. 5:20–21, Paul continues his statement that law came to increase sinfulness by adding: "But where sin increased, grace abounded all the more, so that, as sin reigned in death, grace also might reign through righteousness to eternal life through Jesus Christ our Lord." In his Letter to the Galatians, Paul even contends that "Christ redeemed us from the curse of the law, having become a curse for us" (Gal. 3:13). The law leads and urges us toward Christ, and it was "our custodian until Christ came" (Gal. 3:24). The law was our tutor or governor, as the term "custodian" can also be translated, and kept us under the tutelage and yoke until we were released into freedom through Christ. Christ shows us that the law is not God's final word and the whole content of the Christian proclamation.

Though the gospel stands alongside the law, each has an entirely different function. The gospel proclaims that God's will has already been met in Christ. It shows us a gracious God who meets us in Christ and who forgives us our sins. Paul expresses this eloquently when he says: "But now the righteousness of God has been manifested apart from law, although the law and the prophets bear witness to it" (Rom. 3:21). God's righteousness has been met substitutionally in the life and destiny of Jesus Christ. It is now evident that God wants the redemption of his people and not their destruction.

It would be wrong to assume that the gospel of redemption is confined to the Christ-event. The righteousness of God has its prehistory in the law and the prophets, as Paul reminds us when he says that "the law and the prophets bear witness to it." The Old Testament already testifies to the gracious love of God which culminates in the life and destiny of Christ. Karl Barth picked up this insight in his famous paper of 1935 on "Gospel and Law." By reversing their sequence, he wants to point out that "the law is in the Gospel, comes from the Gospel and is directed to the Gospel."[4] If we want to understand the law, we must first of all know about the gospel.

Barth admits that God's word contains both law and gospel. Since the law is identical with God's will, we have access to it only in Jesus Christ in whom God's word comes audibly to us. "When we see here the will of God being done, when, that is, we see His grace in action, the law is manifested to us."[5] When we perceive God's grace, we realize what the law actually demands. "The law, then, is in the Gospel as the tables of Sinai were in the ark of the covenant."[6] Barth even says that "the law is nothing else than the necessary form of the Gospel, whose content is grace." We are reminded here somewhat of Augustine's style of argumentation when he defined evil both as a deficiency of the good and as a necessary tool that helps us through its contrast to perceive the good. But Barth reverses Augustine's argument by claiming that the goodness of the gospel makes us realize our depravity and sinfulness so that we cling to the gospel. Barth defines the law as a form of the gospel since it bears witness to the gospel. He claims that the sequence of law first and then gospel is only legitimate if we would first look at Christ who reveals himself through the law as our Savior. Knowing that Christ affirms God's valid but misused law, we perceive our shortcomings and flee to God's grace revealed in Christ who fulfills the demands of the law. For Barth, the proper sequence is gospel-law-gospel instead of law-gospel.

The traditional sequence of law first and then gospel that Barth attacks is not foolproof since it might leave the impression that it is synonymous with the succession of Old and New Testaments. Yet Barth's own preference of gospel, law, and gospel is even more misleading since it envelops the law with the gospel and obscures the fact that law and gospel are the same word of God. One cannot divide God's word into the words of law and the words of gospel. Whether we encounter law or gospel depends on how God's word meets us, as condemnation or as confirmation. If we envelop God's demand in his grace, his word loses its seriousness, and we would be in danger of offering cheap grace. Luther rightly stated that the proclamation of the law is the indispensable and necessary presupposition for preaching the gospel. Without the law we would not recognize our own sinfulness but remain secure and proud of our moral capacity. In this way the law is God's alien work which allows us to appreciate the gospel as his proper work. While they function quite differently, law and gospel are certainly the same word of God.

We have seen that the distinction between law and gospel is not identical with that between the Pentateuch or the Old Testament on the one hand and the proclamation of Jesus or the New Testament kergyma on the other. Yet the law can certainly denote the Pentateuch or even the whole Israelite system of law.

At Jesus' time, many Jews had turned God's word into a code of human regulations to assure their righteousness before God. The law had evolved into a self-assertive, legalistic, human system interposing itself between God and humanity and leading to a wrong understanding of human righteousness. Jesus addressed this situation in the Sermon on the Mount and in many other discourses. Today the attitude of many people is similar. They lead ethically virtuous lives and assume that their lives, though short of perfection, will ultimately be met with divine approval. The German poet Wolfgang Goethe summed up well this popular sentiment in his dramatic poem "Faust" when he declared: "Who e'er aspiring, struggles on, for him there is salvation."[7] Yet such an understanding of the law will not lead to freedom. It will utimately enslave people since it suggests that they are righteous though they are not. People will devote themselves to impersonal ethical principles—such as the greatest good for the greatest number of people, or freedom and equality for the underprivileged—instead of responding to God's personal will. Often these self-righteous attempts result in new barriers of injustice and inequality. Law divorced from the gospel can easily turn into a self-serving and self-justifying philosophy. People exchange the living will of God for ethical norms which they attempt to fulfill in order to justify their behavior.

Since people sin by turning their attention to the law instead of to God himself, we must remind them that they actually avoid God and replace him by other norms. We must bring them to repentance through God's word that encounters them as his accusing law and not as their self-designed plan. According to Luther, this demanding and accusing word of God can meet us anywhere in such different items as, for instance, the rustling leaves of a tree and the Lord's Prayer. Each of the petitions in the Lord's Prayer can be perceived as a demand that reminds us of our imperfection. But the same word of God can also encounter us as gospel. For example, Luther assures us that there is much gospel contained in the first commandment since there God promises his faithfulness. We also remember that the so-called Old Testament law originally served as gospel, as the pledge of God's faithfulness to which the Israelites were asked to respond. Only through the constant failure to respond has the law assumed an accusing function.

God's same word can meet us as law or gospel, as demand or as promise. But there is an irreversible movement from law to gospel. If we grasp the gospel in faith, we know about God's acceptance; and the condemning and accusing function of the law vanishes. The gospel has replaced the law; and, consequently, we recognize God in an entirely different light. He no longer appears to us as a righteous God who demands compliance with his will, but as a gracious God who forgives us our trespasses for Christ's sake. If the gospel makes such a difference in our perception of God's word, the question emerges whether or not law still has any validity for the Christian.

THE WORD AS GUIDANCE (THIRD USE AND PENANCE)

If it is true that Christ is the end of the law, as Paul claims, then the law should no longer be of any concern for us Christians. Yet such quick discarding of the law would conflict with Jesus' claim that he did not come to abolish the law but to fulfill it. Indeed, it was the conviction of the New Testament writers that Christ fulfilled God's will substitutionally. This did not mean that the law had lost its validity for us as God's guiding will or as his accusing law. If it had, we would either live in the immediacy of God and have no need of any mediated guidance, or we would be totally sinless without need for repentance and renewal. Since we still live in this world and succumb to its sinfulness, we need guidance and repentance. Thus God's law meets us in its third use, the use for the reborn; and it also meets us in the Office of the Keys, that is, in penance.

The third use of the law has occasionally been disputed, especially since Luther did not explicitly mention such use. But it was evident to most Reformers and even to Luther himself that the law is not without significance for the Christian. The emphasis on the third use is particularly strong in the Reformed tradition. For instance, Calvin claimed that "The third and principal use, which pertains more closely to the proper purpose of the law, finds its place among believers in whose hearts the Spirit of God already lives and reigns."[8] A similar line of thought was pursued by Philip Melanchthon, the Lutheran *Book of Concord*, and the theologians of Lutheran orthodoxy. It is interesting that Calvin introduces the third use of the law primarily with quotations from the Old Testament. For instance, he quotes the psalmist saying: "Thy word is a lamp to my feet and a light to my path" (Ps. 119:105), and another time: "The law of the Lord is perfect, reviving the soul" (Ps. 19:7).

Christians certainly need moral directives and guidelines; they need to hear God's will to order their lives. Yet once we are confronted with the gospel and understand the full implications of God's gracious will, our response does not come from the pressure of the law. Christians live up to the law, not because of certain demands, but because they love God and appreciate his righteousness. Yet in its original intention, not even the Old Testament law can be properly interpreted as a coaxing or urging institution. For instance, the Ten Commandments are not introduced with the assertion that this is what God demands. They are introduced with the reminder that this is what God has done for you. First they tell us what God has done for Israel: "I am the Lord your God, who brought you out of the land of Egypt, out of the house of bondage" (Exod. 20:2). The commandment to love one's neighbor is introduced in a similar way: "You shall love your neighbor as yourself: I am the Lord" (Lev. 19:18). Because God is gracious to us, we are called to transfer his love to our neighbor. In the Old Testament God's word was originally intended as gospel and not as prescribing or condemning word. It was to show us the kind of God we have and to evoke our response, a response freely given. Being justified children of God, we do the will of God and want what God wants us to do. Of course, such response to God's will is not without any guidance.

We acknowledge the existence of commandments in the Bible that serve as guiding moral directives. It would be potentially misleading, however, to regard them as law in terms of a civil or even convicting use. They depict an evangelical use in the original sense of the divine command. They do not express a demanding commandment in the sense of "you shall . . . ," but invite us, "you may because. . . ." They serve as guidelines in our attempt to meet the will of God, and they are not set as legal devices that might assure a righteous life. Christians are no longer oriented toward the law, but portray an almost oscillating existence conducting their lives under the freedom of the gospel, yet still prone to seek their own ways. They do not suddenly find themselves in the state of the redeemed beyond the possibility of sinning. Paul sensed this too when he used frequent imperatives to show that the Christian existence is still marked by temptation and sin. Luther described the same situation when he characterized a Christian as sinner and justified at the same time.

Being a Christian justified before God does not induce an ontological change. But it is indicative of a new relationship with God. This relationship is always subject to change and must be continually regained. When we lapse into sin God's word turns for us into law to drive us back to the gospel. Thus in the Christian community it does not suffice to proclaim the gospel alone. Because of our sinful behavior, it must be supplemented by preaching the law. As justified Christians we live without the law; but as sinners we live under it, and it drives us back to the gracious God.

Since God remains with us through the law, the severing of our relationship with God is never bilateral. Even as lapsed ones we stay and remain Christians. The promise of the gospel does not become void once we turn our backs on God. His gracious word continues to stand, and we always have the opportunity of returning to him. As Christians we do not live under the thumb of God, but are called to freedom as his sons and daughters. While this freedom is not without limits, it would be inappropriate to call these limits law. We should rather call them orders and guidelines that allow us to live responsibly. In their sinfulness Christians are confronted with a convicting use of the law. In their daily lives they attempt to fulfill the civil use. But as new people of God they respond freely to his will and no longer live under compulsion and pressure. The guidance provided to channel their response should not be called law but, as Paul Althaus suggested, divine command.[9] In this category we could also classify the New Testament exhortations concerning the Christian life (*Haustafeln*).

The distinction between law and gospel assumes a peculiar form in the Office of the Keys or the practice of confession and absolution. Roman Catholic tradition considers penance a sacrament which includes the Office of the Keys. Lutherans, however, closely associate penance with the sacraments but do not actually consider it one. For instance, in the Augsburg Confession, penance is located after baptism and Holy Communion, and in Luther's Small Catechism is placed after baptism and before the Lord's Supper. This indicates its close affinity to the sacraments proper without actually giving it sacramental status. In his Apology of the Augsburg Confession, Philip Melanchthon even states that penance is one of the three sacraments. Yet this suggestion has not been picked up by other Protestants. The Calvinist tradition, too, refuses to consider confession and absolution a sacrament. We will have to pursue further the question of what constitutes a sacrament. At this point it suffices to state that Protestants do not perceive penance as a sacrament. They rightly see that confession and absolution are intimately connected with the proclamation of law and gospel as the one word of God.

When we briefly survey the main passages in the New Testament that elucidate the function of the Office of the Keys, we notice a significant development. We hear in connection with Jesus' words to Peter that on this rock we build his church: "I will give you the keys of the kingdom of heaven, and whatever you bind on earth shall be bound in heaven, and whatever you loose on earth shall be loosed in heaven" (Matt. 16:19). Peter is entrusted here with binding and loosing people on earth; this means with excluding and accepting them into the Christian community. In the Gospel of John, this function is now extended to all the disciples and is understood more theologically as remission of sins. So we hear Jesus say to his disciples: "Receive the Holy Spirit. If you forgive the sins of any, they are forgiven; if you retain the sins of any, they are retained" (John 20:22–23). The Christian community, or at least the Twelve, understood themselves to succeed Peter in the Office of the Keys. This is already obvious from Matt. 18:18 where the exercise of this office is no longer restricted to Peter. There Jesus is saying to his disciples: "Truly, I say to you, whatever you bind on earth shall be bound in heaven, and whatever you loose on earth shall be loosed in heaven."

The Office of the Keys is intimately connected with the proclamation of God's word. There is a parallel between listening to God's word and receiving forgiveness of sins. When Jesus sent out the disciples he admonished them: "And if any one will not receive you or listen to your words, shake off the dust from your feet as you leave that house or town. Truly, I say to you, it shall be more tolerable on the day of judgment for the land of Sodom and Gomorrah than for that town" (Matt. 10:14–15). The reception of God's word decides over life and death, and those who are charged with its proclamation shall symbolize this by shaking off the dust from their feet as a sign that they have separated themselves from those who rejected God's word. The ultimate consequences of the proclamation of God's word are to be made known to its listeners. The Office of the Keys is based on the pronouncement of law and gospel as the one word of God. Our response to this word has definite consequences, and those who pronounce the word are empowered to make known these consequences to the listeners by absolving them or leaving them in their sins. Since penance is inextricably connected with God's word, the public proclamation of this word and the use of penance are administered by the same persons. For instance, similar to its hierarchical teaching order, the Roman Catholic Church has a hierarchical order for administering various degrees of penance.

The Office of the Keys should never be considered in purely administrative terms. It is exercised on behalf of God so that the sinner be saved and not perish. It is not a convenient means to enforce authoritarian decisions. Those who handle penance do this on behalf of the Lord of the church and not in the name of human authorities.

Since proclamation and penance are inseparable, the church has realized that the one-time remission of sins through baptism cannot be the end of the penitential process. We are in need of continuous forgiveness. Martin Luther expressed this well when he stated in connection with his explanation of baptism in his Small Catechism: "The old Adam in us, together with all sins and evil lusts, should be drowned by daily sorrow and repentance and be put to death, and that the new man should come forth daily and rise up, cleansed and righteous, to live forever in God's presence."[10] Confession and absolution is a daily process and cannot be confined to special occasions when one has committed especially grave sin. This is also apparent from Luther's Ninety-five Theses where he claimed at the outset: "When our Lord and Master Jesus Christ said, 'Repent' [Matt. 4:17], he willed the entire life of believers to be one of repentance."[11]

There is also a controversy surrounding penitence that is similar to the one we have seen concerning the third use of the law. In the Roman Catholic tradition, there are three parts to that penitential process—contrition, confession, and satisfaction. Lutherans, however, see contrition and confession as sufficient (cf. CA 11 and 12). While Luther rejected the imposition of satisfaction as administered by the clergy in his Ninety-five Theses, he insisted that "inner repentance is worthless unless it produces various outward mortifications of the flesh." There is no law that can spell out what kind of restitution would have to be made in each case. Yet even if there were, we can never completely undo a sinful act since we are unable to reverse history. Only God who sets history into motion and has it under his control can effect restitution in the true sense. This does not mean that we should lean back and simply do nothing. Once we receive forgiveness, we need ethical guidance showing us how to respond properly to the grace freely received. Satisfaction is not a new law or a demand, but an opportunity to restore that part of God's creation which we willfully impaired through our sinful activities. If this opportunity is not grasped, Luther is right that even the most convincing "inner repentance is worthless."

While the Roman Catholic Church still emphasizes individual confession in the confessional, the Lutheran rejection of a legalistic confessional practice and the discovery of the autonomy of the individual conscience have almost brought private confession to extinction in Protestant churches. The usual Protestant form is that of corporate confession, especially in preparation for the Lord's Supper. While corporate confession receives the same liberating word as private confession, it too can become a matter of routine. Thus this practice also has to be continuously checked to retain its seriousness.

Modern psychotherapy has shown us the significance of a one-to-one dialogue. We have learned how an unreconciled past and suppressed guilt feelings can literally haunt us. They can cause feelings of inadequacy, lead to anger and aggression, or even result in serious mental and bodily disorders. In a one-to-one dialogue we can bring our house in order, uncover the deepest reasons for our wrongdoings and subsequent ill-feelings, and can more accurately judge the severity of our sinfulness. While largely depending on our individual cooperation, psychotherapy can make us work through our past and overcome a negative self-image. While such work should not be underestimated, private confession can go one important step further by pointing to Jesus Christ who frees and forgives the penitent sinner. It is Christ's liberating word as it is pronounced to us that constitutes the biggest difference between Christian confession and secular self-help attempts. While in secular therapies we can at most improve ourselves by uncovering our past and reconciling ourselves with it, as Christians we are allowed to confess our wrongdoings and then start anew. The liberating word is directed to us in an unmistakable way.

While the process of confession can be ritualized in an actual order of private confession and absolution, it can also take on the form of a counseling session in which the confessor, usually the pastor, can guide us in our reappropriation of the past and in so doing lead us to the Christ who frees us from our past. In a less structured way Christ's forgiving word can also meet us in the mutual conversation and consolation of fellow Christians (Matt. 18:15ff.), perhaps the earliest form of penance. God's Word, which hardly ever meets us immediately, can meet us there through another person in a reprimanding, freeing, and guiding way.

While it is often difficult to start anew considering the possible public impact of our wrongdoings and the unwillingness of others to forgive us, we may, however, be assured that in the eyes of God we are new persons. Justified through confession and absolution we are totally justified in God's memory and estimation. God will not hold our past against us. In confession and absolution we receive the entire forgiveness of all our sins. This does not hold true just for one time in our lives, as the church initially thought regarding penance, but whenever we come back to God as contrite sinners who ask for forgiveness and seriously intend to amend our ways.

God's liberating and forgiving word cannot be taken lightly. It asks for our response as new beings, a response that should be expressive of our newly found union with God. Since God does not treat us as puppets, but appeals to our freedom, this underscores the necessity of our response. If such a response is not forthcoming, or if repentance is not initiated as far as we can ascertain, it might be necessary that so-called church sanctions be imposed on the unrepentant sinner. These sanctions—for instance, exclusion from certain offices or activities in the Christian community—should always be administered to the benefit of the punished. The movement from law to grace must always prevail. Though they should never be administered too quickly, church sanctions are not relics of medieval authoritarianism. They are an offer of grace through the administration of the law. Since God is a God of grace, sinners are not punished to perish but that they might amend their lives and live.

EXCURSUS: WHERE GOD'S WORD MEETS THE PEOPLE

When we talk about the judging, liberating, and guiding word, we must also ask where this word encounters us today. Especially in the prophetic writings of the Old Testament we hear that the word of God was addressed to specific persons. This kind of immediacy of God's word through auditions, dreams, and other media is still a present reality. Whether God's word is reliably related through such "direct" messages must be judged by comparing them with the God-disclosive history. If they fall within the bounds of that word which has occurred during God's history with his people we may be relatively sure that the "new" word is not the result of a misunderstanding or deliberate distortion. Thus the claim: "God told me," must be judged by the common tradition of God's self-disclosure in history in order to safeguard it against fraud (cf. Matt. 24:11). Since Jesus Christ is God's final word, any "new" word of God cannot surpass his self-disclosure in Jesus Christ. It can, however, assist us in appropriating this self-disclosure in a more current way. Thus God's prophetic word spoken to us today will help us to better discern his way and fulfill his will.

When we mentioned that a "new" word must be judged by the God-disclosive history, we are referring to the most common source for our knowledge of God's word, the written reflection upon his self-disclosure, or simply the Bible as the written word. Karl Barth rightly reminded us that it is not sufficient simply to read the written word in private devotions or in public worship service. We must also discern *the* word in the words and discover its existential meaning for us which meets us as demand, comfort, or guidance. Without the continuous search for the word in the words, the Bible remains a dry and ineffectual document relating to us a distant history about foreign people instead of becoming a living voice of the gospel which frees, upbuilds, and guides us. Certainly we should use the most modern tools today available to exegete the word. But a mere discovery of grammatical peculiarities and different layers of tradition does not yet touch upon the essence of the written document. We must look for the different ways and contexts in which the message itself is presented there and then ask whether and how that message will speak to us today.

The hermeneutical question of how the text is to be translated into today's language and context is decisive for unlocking God's word for our time. We should take heed, however, that the translation process actually unlocks the message and does not become a science in itself which prevents the text from disclosing its contents. The temptation to cast the text into a preconceived mold which predetermines what the text can say is great. As Rudolf Bultmann insisted, we must always be open for the possibility that the text itself may challenge and change our own prior understanding of it. God's word is always causing surprises and beckoning us to a new assessment of ourselves and our situation.

Especially in the Protestant tradition the word encounters us most often as the preached word. Again this word can meet us as law, gospel, or guidance. Since the preached word is God's word spoken anew into our situation, several cautions must be noted:

1. The preached word dare not be degraded to espousing one's own opinions and preferences. The preached word is God's own word and not that of the preacher. Therefore one's own opinion must be clearly designated as such and occupy a secondary place.

2. The preached word does not consist of expounding one's own favorite Bible passages but must contain the whole counsel of God. The best methods for avoiding a sermon on the word of one's own choice is to follow prescribed texts such as in lectionaries of the main Christian tradition.

3. The preached word must comprise the whole word of God. While it is neither desirable nor possible to narrate the whole history of salvation in one sermon, a preacher dare not dwell only on certain portions of Scripture. As the narrated word in the worship service contains Gospel, epistle, and an Old Testament reading, the preached word should also draw from the whole Bible and not only from selected portions.

4. Similarly, the preached word cannot dwell on the law alone without becoming oppressive and condemning. It dare not dwell on God's grace

alone either without offering cheap grace, and eventually even the milk of human kindness, instead of the liberating grace of the gospel. It also should not provide guidance alone lest it become merely another kind of "advice for better living" and in so doing become overly law-oriented. Though it is most desirable to present a proper balance between law and gospel in each sermon, one worship service never stands by itself. It is part of a series of worship experiences. Therefore one sermon may tend more toward law, another more toward the gospel, or toward guidance. Yet the overall picture should provide a balanced presentation of the whole counsel of God.

5. Since the preached word speaks to specific people in their specific situations, it dare not be exchanged for an abstract theological treatise fitted for all times, places, and seasons. So-called canned sermons especially run the risk of turning the word of God into an abstract and timeless truth instead of preaching the living word of the gospel. The preached word must address the audience in such a way that the individual listeners can identify themselves with the message and the situation to which it speaks. This presupposes familiarity with the people and the conditions in which they live.

6. Since the preached word is not a dialogical word as we encounter it in an individual counseling situation, the preacher should take care not to single out individual people and address them personally with God's judging, liberating, and guiding word. Singling out individuals confuses the public and corporate identity of the worshiping community with the private and individualized situation of the one who needs counseling and advice. This mistake may result in embarrassment for the individual and have the consequence that he or she will try to shield themselves against the destructive effects of a misappropriated word.

Since the preached word forms the corporate identity of the people of God, it is the prime tool for bringing them together in solidarity, mutual concern, and support. It also shapes their self-understanding as Christians in an almost unsurpassable way. Since it pronounces God's word for today it is also the most prominent tool for evangelism: confronting people with God's word and inviting them to accept Christ as their Lord and Savior by dedicating their lives to him.

THE DIALOGICAL WORD (PRAYER AND LITURGY)

We have noticed several times that God's word invites our response. We are not confronted with God in an impersonal way, similar to the laws of nature, or to a merciless fate. God wants and establishes a dialogue with us, as is shown in the New Testament by the many exhortations to pray. For instance, we hear: "Ask, and it will be given you; seek, and you will find; knock, and it will be opened to you" (Matt. 7:7). This dialogue is expressed primarily in two ways, in a more formalized and ritualized way in liturgy (adoration as liturgy) and in a less formal and often spontaneous manner in prayer (adoration as prayer). The main distinction between prayer and liturgy lies in their comprehensiveness. While liturgy always includes moments of prayer, the latter does not necessarily include moments of liturgy.

We can distinguish many different kinds of prayer: corporate and individual, free and formalized, and intercessory and doxological. The fundamental presupposition of prayer is that God wants to engage in a dialogue with us. It is further presupposed that there is a certain realm of freedom in which prayer can unfold its activity. If these presuppositions were not met, prayer would be nothing but an attempt to calm our nerves or to obtain self-control, an approach often used in Far Eastern meditation exercises. Since God is our dialogue partner in prayer, we should not address him in a carefree, casual attitude. We also should not pray in a boasting attitude convinced that God has no choice but to agree with the contents of our prayers (Matt. 6:5–7). A prayer should be precise and to the point but offered in humility. For instance, the Lord's Prayer which Jesus taught his disciples begins with the affirmation of God's holiness, and it concludes with the doxology (Matt. 6:9–13). The emphasis on God's holiness informs our attitude in prayer as well as its content. When we hear Jesus say that "whatever you ask the Father in my name, he may give it to you" (John 15:16), this does not mean that God will give us everything for which we ask him. Dietrich Bonhoeffer elucidated well the meaning of this often misunderstood passage when he commented: "God does not give us everything we want, but he does fulfil all his promises."[12]

Prayer is not a frivolous attempt to discover how far-reaching God's power is—whether he can suspend the law of gravity or reverse the sequence of day and night. It is rather the reliance on the promise expressed in the Psalms: "Call upon me in the day of trouble; I will deliver you, and you shall glorify me" (Ps. 50:15). Christ has overcome the destructive and anti-godly powers; and we, as his followers, are encouraged to call upon God to deliver us and others from the impact of these powers. Through our prayers, we are on God's side, cooperating and dialoguing with him about the future of the world. Martin Luther was right when he called God's order or command and the prayers of the Christians the two pillars that support the entire world and without which the world would disintegrate.[13]

Prayer can have many contents. The most appropriate approach to God as the Wholly Other is that of adoration and praise. We should not only call upon God as some kind of security blanket or as a genie in a bottle. We should thank him for his help and protection, acknowledge his continual support, and praise him as our Creator, Sustainer, and Redeemer. If we cease to pray, our life is no longer in tune with the source of life; we cut ourselves off from God and assume we are self-sufficient. Prayer as adoration and praise makes us recall the one from whom we have everything. We acknowledge our dependency and do not take anything for granted such as good health, good weather, a job, our family, etc.

Most of our prayers do not focus primarily on adoration but on petitions and intercessions. Since God invited us to dialogue with him, it is only proper that we bring before him all our anxieties and personal afflictions such as sickness, economic and family problems, and even our sinful aversions from God. There is no need to suppress any petitions whether they envision eternal or temporal goals. But petitional prayers are more than presenting God with a shopping list. An essential part of Christian prayer is to seek God's forgiveness for past and present sins and to find hope for the future. If we do not include in our prayers the plea for forgiveness of sins, our dialogue with God will be tarnished by estrangement. The quest for forgiveness will also include reference to our petitions and intercessions to discern whether they result from our own sinful and selfish interests or whether they were done to conform with God's will. Often prayers are only the result of piously disguised selfishness attempting to impose our desires on God's work. Thus petitions must first be concerned with renewal and inner strength. But petitional prayers include more than forgiveness. We will ask for inner peace and tranquillity in times of conflict, clarity of outlook, new strength at moments of fatigue, and power to cope with the daily demands of life.

We might ask why we should expect God to answer our prayers or to help us in times of need. Here the life and destiny of Jesus serves as the great paradigm to understand God's action. Since God has acted benevolently toward us in Christ, we can expect that he will again act so toward us if we ask him. God cared about us little and insignificant beings so much that he came to us in the human form of Jesus Christ. As we hear in the Magnificat, he puts down the mighty from their seats and lifts up those who are in low esteem (Luke 1:52).

Considering petitional prayers, we should not forget the frequent petitions for physical health and healing from disease. We must express caution here, however, against the idea that prayers induce some kind of magic that could substitute for adequate medical care or ward off undesirable events. Appropriate care and prayer are not mutually exclusive. Prayer (dialogue with God) and action (a result of that dialogue) are appropriate ways in which we can engage in the affairs of the world. When we consider petitions concerning events in nature, we will usually affirm the protective orders of God and will not ask him frivolously to reverse the sequence of the seasons or to bring about other strange constellations. Yet it is part of our task as God's dialogue partners to remind him of those who are especially exposed to the dangers of nature such as travelers, sailors, pilots, and miners. Again, prayers are not intended to replace protective measures, but to accompany and perhaps enhance them. In a similar way, it is our prerogative and duty to pray for good harvest, and to remind God of adverse conditions, such as floods, storms, and other disasters in nature so that their impact will be softened or perhaps averted.

Since prayer should not be a selfish action, we will keep in mind the well-being of others as much as of ourselves. The same adoration, praise, and petitions that we extend on our behalf, we extend on behalf of others. Since prayers take the hope of fulfillment from the way God acted in Jesus Christ, their limits, too, should come from Jesus Christ. They should always conclude with the express admission with which the evangelist tells us Jesus concluded his prayer in Gethsemane: "Nevertheless, not as I will, but as thou wilt" (Matt. 26:39). A Christian prayer is not a demand for God's surrender, but the prerogative and duty of dialogue with the one who formed the earth and the whole universe and who has been our dwelling place in all generations (Ps. 90:1–2).

When we now briefly consider the liturgy, we are at once struck by a considerable change in the meaning of the word "liturgy." In popular Greek, liturgy denoted a responsible public office, a duty, or a service, performed at one's own expense. In the Septuagint, the Greek translation of the Old Testament, liturgy is used to translate the Hebrew *sheret* ("priestly service") (cf. Num. 4:12; Exod. 28:35, etc.). In the New Testament the term is used only a few times with varying meanings. Significant for us is Acts 13:2, however, because there we notice that a prayer service is called liturgy. Especially since the fourth century, the term liturgy was used to denote the Christian cult and its main actions, above all the celebration of the Eucharist. In the orthodox tradition the holy liturgy is synonymous with the eucharistic celebration.

While the liturgy is in many ways formalized dialogue, it also includes moments of spontaneity (e.g., the preached word, exchange of peace, prayers). The dialogue proceeds on two levels, between the congregation and the minister(s) and between the worshiping community and God. Intrinsic to every liturgy are prayers, usually at least the Lord's Prayer, and readings from the New and Old Testaments. In many ways liturgy is reenactment of God's saving action, especially its high points, such as the exodus from Egypt, the passion history, or the rescue of Noah. Through this reenactment of history, people are initiated and reminded of God's activities with his people, including his fundamental promises. Liturgy also involves the people in the reenactment process by responding to and participating in it. Often there are ritual actions, such as the sacraments, through which the faithful participate in God's promises and through which these promises are remembered and appropriated.

Since in liturgy the main portions of salvation history are being reenacted, liturgy must also be understood as dramatized word. God's promissory word, made manifest in history, is being recalled and re-presented in worship. The reenactment of the drama of salvation can be enhanced through highly formalized speech and the use of music. The narration can be done in the form of chanting, either by the minister(s) alone or in dialogue with the congregation. It can be underscored by the musical accompaniment or through congregational singing of hymns, which themselves often narrate parts of salvation history, or even through special musical presentations. Since the Reformers emphasized the primacy of the preached word, many Protestant denominations have created rich treasures of hymns and other church music. We should note here the famous oratorios of George Frederick Handel and the organ works of Johann Sebastian Bach. We should also not forget Bach's famous passions in which the passion stories of the evangelists are retold in song with the support of orchestral music. Today quite often choirs enhance the liturgy and the proclamation of the word by underscoring with musical renderings the major theme of the day or of the season. Thus within the liturgy many different art forms have been developed from Gregorian chant to spirituals and a cappella choirs.

Since the heart of the Christian liturgy is the Eucharist, a festive and concurrently solemn note is appropriate. We celebrate the resurrection of Christ which includes the mystery of the cross as its presupposition and point of departure. The reason for joy and celebration is based on Christ's victory over death and the promise of new life connected with it. Since God's action is constitutive of the Christian liturgy we realize that liturgy is in its deepest sense not a human product, but something we receive and reenact in worship. The Christian liturgy stands in succession to the liturgy of ancient Israel. We need not be surprised therefore that many of its particular forms of expression find their precedence in the Israel of old; yet the content is shaped by God's decisive action in Jesus Christ.

Liturgy, though guided and led by the minister(s), involves the whole worshiping community with all its senses. The bodily movements within the liturgy, such as genuflection, turning to the altar, walking to the pulpit, processing, etc., are means to emphasize the different parts of the liturgy. Similarly, colors signify certain festivals or seasons of the year which recall God's activities. Liturgical gowns underscore the different functions of the persons involved (choirs, acolytes, presiding minister, assistants, etc.) and the kind of duties they perform. Since liturgy is intimately connected with God's word and action, it remembers his deeds, witnesses to his presence, and expects his final coming which will culminate in the redemption of his promises. Liturgy flows out of God's word and action and symbolizes them realistically through word and action. In the liturgy we are drawn into the dialogue between God and the worshiping community. We explain our predicament and implore his help; he in turn shows us what he has done, is doing, and will do. Since God is acting through the liturgical process, liturgy has a sacramental and at the same time a miraculous aspect.

THE EMPIRICAL WORD (MIRACLES)

Nowhere are word and action more closely intertwined than in miracles. While forgiveness and judgment also imply immediate action, the empirical side of these actions (forgiveness of sins or condemning someone) are usually removed from empirical investigation. Even the gospels admit this, as shown in the story of the paralytic (Mark 2:1–12). When Jesus announced to him that his sins were forgiven, immediately the factuality of this deed was questioned. Jesus countered: "Which is easier, to say to the paralytic, 'Your sins are forgiven,' or to say, 'Rise, take up your pallet and walk'? But that you may know that the Son of man has authority on earth to forgive sins . . . I say to you, 'rise, take up your pallet and go home' " (Mark 2:9–11).

A miracle seems to show immediately the empirical consequences of what the word entails. Yet people are not always convinced that a miracle has indeed happened and that its author is definitely disclosed. For instance, some believed that Jesus had performed miracles through God's power, others accused him of being connected with the devil, and a third group remained totally indifferent to his deeds. This means that a miracle is not like a magic act that would demonstrate the power of the magician or of the source of magic. Miracles are also not demonstrations of God's power that should convince the onlookers who is in control of things.

According to the biblical witnesses, miracles are intrinsically related to God's salvational promises. At the high points of salvation history, we are confronted with miracles such as the parting of the Red Sea, the virginal conception of Jesus, or his resurrection as the Christ. Of course, one could object that miracles are just literary devices to translate Jesus' proclamation into sign language. Thus there might be no historical reality that pertains to them. Yet today even the severest critics of the New Testament sources admit that Jesus did indeed perform acts that his contemporaries regarded as miraculous and that we still consider highly unusual.

Jesus' miracles are not without analogies. For some of his contemporaries, miracles are reported that show an astounding similarity with those of Jesus. Most prominent is Apollonius of Tyana, an itinerant Neo-Pythagorean teacher, who is supposed to have raised people from the dead and healed many who were sick. In antiquity some of the miracles may simply have been attributed to certain people to emphasize their significance. It should also be noted that the New Testament witnesses even relate other miracle stories, and they are convinced that performing miracles was not the exclusive prerogative of Jesus. They tell us that Jesus himself warned of false Christs and of prophets at the end time who would perform great signs and wonders (Mark 13:22). The apostles, too, knew of people who used sorcery to perform miraculous deeds (cf. Acts 8:9).

Since Jesus' miracles are closely tied to his proclamation, it is insufficient to interpret them exclusively in the light of Near Eastern or Greco-Roman thought. We must understand them primarily in the light of his message. If it were his stated goal to announce and to bring about the kingdom of God, then his miracles are signs and proleptic anticipation of the kingdom. Miracles are signs to illustrate his message, but they are not means to demonstrate his power and to legitimate him as they quite often do for other people (cf. Matt. 12:38–39). They show the truthfulness of God's promises, that he is actively involved in the creative process and does not simply confirm the present course of affairs but is willing to give it a new and unexpected turn.

This involvement results in a decisive confrontation with those powers that want to destroy his creation. We read in the New Testament that Jesus claimed he was authorized by God to fight and overcome the destructive powers. Through Jesus' miracles God validated

Jesus' claim, he overcame these powers and initiated a completely new order. The destructive and anti-godly powers were forced to retreat at one specific point at which the miracle was performed. As sick people are returned to health, dead are brought back to life, biologically impairing phenomena such as hunger are overcome, and physically limiting phenomena such as space and gravity are eliminated, we obtain glimpses of an entirely new creation. Miracles are signs that the announcement of the commencing kingdom and of the reign of God will indeed be enacted. What the seer in the Book of Revelation still envisions for the time of eschatological perfection has become proleptic reality in the miracles of Jesus. "Death shall be no more, neither shall there be mourning nor crying nor pain any more, for the former things have passed away" (Rev. 21:4).

Jesus' miracles are only temporary points of victory over the anti-godly powers. The people healed were again afflicted by diseases, those brought back to life died again, and those he fed became hungry again. Jesus was not essentially helpless against the present structure of reality, so that he could at best provide temporary help against the evils of this world. On the contrary, his miracles concur with his message and indicate that the present reality will be transformed into a new, undistorted reality, the new creation. The confidence for this assertion is not derived from his message alone but above all from his resurrection. When God resurrected Jesus as the Christ through the power of the Spirit, Jesus never died again. In Jesus' resurrection, death was permanently, though proleptically, overcome through a new form of life (1 Cor. 15:55–57). In Jesus God's word has come true in its fullest sense. The promised and hoped-for transformation of the whole cosmos had commenced. It was not simply a restoration, as a resuscitation phenomenon would indicate, but the showing forth and anticipation of a new cosmos. Since the inauguration of a new reality happened in and with Jesus, its consequences extend far beyond the person of Jesus. God vindicated Jesus as the one whom he said he was, the bringer of new life and the Messiah. This means that his resurrection gave his proclamation new credibility. We can now accept his proclamation, his miracles, and the miracles still being performed in his name as signposts foreshadowing and depicting a new world to come.

Concurring with his message, the miracles have eschatological quality. They point to a promised eschaton and anticipate proleptically the new world order that they introduce. They indicate that our present world is not endowed with permanence but is on its way to a new world. The present order will give way to a new order of perfection. The unexpected character of the miracles also shows us that there is no developmental continuity between the present state of affairs and the new world to come. Salvation is neither continuation of the fallen creation on a higher level nor development toward the promised goal. Only something unprecedented and new, as it is foreshadowed in the miracles, can bring about the desired goal. This does not mean a discarding of the present and complete discontinuity. But there will be a total restructuring of the present that will eliminate current distortions such as pain, alienation, and decay, and will allow for new life in the immediacy of God.

When we assign such importance to the resurrection of Christ, we must caution that none of the miracles, the resurrection included, has necessarily convincing power in the sense of empirical verification of the veracity of God's promises. Though it is most proper to conclude that God is indeed the actor in Christian miracles, empirical proofs involving claims about ultimacy (i.e., God) are necessarily ambiguous. For instance, Matthew tells us that nobody could deny that the tomb in which Jesus had been laid was again empty. But this fact led to opposite conclusions. While the disciples proclaimed that Jesus had risen, other people disseminated the rumor that his disciples had stolen his corpse by night (Matt. 28:13). Even when Jesus appeared personally to his disciples as the resurrected one, some doubted (Matt. 28:17) and some thought they saw a ghost (Luke 24:37). Though one can ascertain the state prior to a miracle and the state after a miracle has occurred, the miraculous act itself, that is, the transition from the state prior to the state after, is inaccessible to investigation. It does not disclose anything about the nature of the transition itself—whether it is endowed by God with eschatological significance, whether it is a sign that we are confronted with an especially gifted person (such as an actual miracle worker as opposed to a fraud), or whether it is a seductive act of the anti-godly powers intended to pull us away from God. Since a miracle is not an empirical proof of the veracity of God's word, but the proclamation of God's word in sign language, it is susceptible to manipulation and rejection. The scribes and pharisees did not change their minds when they were confronted with the miracle. They heard Jesus' message of the commencement of the salvational process and rejected it together with its signs. Jesus rightly reminded us: "If they do not hear Moses and the prophets, neither will they be convinced if some one should rise from the dead" (Luke 16:31).

Our whole discussion of miracles would be totally obsolete if there were no scientific possibilities for such occurrences. Before we side with those who reject the miracles as being contrary to the laws of nature or with those who assert that God can always interrupt the causal nexus, we should first define what we understand by a miracle. Often the term is used very loosely as in the miracle of communication or the miracle of air transportation or the miracle of modern medicine. But a miracle should denote neither something astounding nor highly complicated. For our purposes a miracle is an act of God which runs counter to our usual sense of experience and which becomes visible in the objective world. A miracle is an exception; something which occurs every day we should not call miracle or novelty. The problem that is posed by a miracle, however, is not its exceptional character, but that it becomes visible in the empirical world.

A miracle is a *mixtum compositum.* As an act of God it pertains to the metaphysical or supernatural dimension, but as something visible it belongs to the natural world. As the natural sciences increased in stature, a more and more stringent distinction was made between the natural and the supernatural realm of God. If God is the agent of a miracle, it is commonly argued, then he will proceed in a supernatural manner and not in a natural one. With this dichotomy between the natural and the supernatural, the potential for conflict existed between those who claimed that the natural context is so all-encompassing that it does not allow for "supernatural" exceptions and others who claim that God can interrupt the natural flow of events whenever he wants. At this point it is interesting to consult Augustine for a definition of how a miracle occurs. He objects to the common notion that miracles could be contrary to nature since both nature and a miracle are by the will of God and since God's will is certainly not self-contradictory. He then asserts that "a portent, therefore, happens not contrary to nature, but contrary to what we know as nature."[14] This means that for him this dichotomy between the natural and the supernatural was not yet given. He still saw the world as a unity governed by God's will in which some items occurred more frequently than others.

It was not even until the ninth century that the term "supernatural" made its appearance in Western theology. Especially from the thirteenth century onward, through the help of Thomas Aquinas, the term supernatural became part of the standard vocabulary in theological circles. For Aquinas, a miracle was defined as something difficult and unusual and something that surpassed the capabilities of nature and the expectations of those who surveyed its course. The first part of this assertion stayed within the definition used by Augustine, while the second one was prone to cause trouble for those asserting the factuality of miracles. It could imply that for normal action nature alone sufficed, whereas for miraculous activities both God and nature were necessary. One might even conclude that God was involved in only supernatural occurrences but not in those of every day. Unintentionally the course was laid out for divorcing God more and more from the natural realm and for relegating him completely to the supernatural sphere.

How much at odds our scientific world view had at one time become with the accounts of the Bible is reflected in Rudolf Bultmann's famous verdict: "It is impossible to use electric light and the wireless and to avail ourselves of modern medical and surgical discoveries, and at the same time to believe in the New Testament world of daemons and spirits."[15]

In recent years, however, scientists have discovered more and more that nature is not ruled by ironclad laws which it must obey. It is no longer tenable to perceive them as laws according to which events must occur, but as laws derived from our experience of the way events generally happen. This means that laws are not determinative of events, but, conversely, events determine the laws which we establish and according to which we expect further events of like nature to occur.

These new insights go hand in hand with the biblical understanding of the efficacy of God's word. Neither the Old nor the New

Testament conceived of God's word as requiring action contrary to or superimposed on nature. Nor was it assumed that these were ironclad laws which God breaks to perform his miracles. For the biblical witnesses the whole world process was the result of God's creative word (Gen. 1:3; etc.), while miracles were the enactment of his promissory word as something new and surprising. God's miraculous activity occurs within and through the present structure of nature. This means that a miracle becomes visible in the natural context insofar as we observe something that runs counter to our usual sense of experience and consequences of which allow it to be perceived as having salvational significance.

Since a miracle is not predictable, we cannot produce it in laboratory environment to analyze all its causes and their interaction. Only once we realize that a miracle has occurred (e.g., the Israelites arrived safely at the other side of the Red Sea while the Egyptians did not), can we attempt to bring the states after and prior to their occurrence into a causal relationship. As scientists, we will not resort to God but only to natural causes to establish their causal relationship. Yet our faith that relies on God being involved in all facets of life will not be satisfied with a completely "natural" explanation. It will perceive that this totally natural event was quite "supernatural." We might question whether a twofold view of nature does not eventually lead to schizophrenia. Of course, we should remember that Jesus himself was a completely human being and that at the same time he was totally divine. The schizophrenia, therefore, could already be contained in this central affirmation of the Christian faith.

In recent years there has been a remarkable advance in the understanding of the structure of nature that seems to ensue in a dual approach to nature. For instance, the Danish physicist Niels Bohr introduced the principle of complementarity, suggesting that wave and particle properties are complementary aspects of a single reality. In a similar way, we might consider the issue of relating mind and brain or mind and body (i.e., is a human being only a biophysical machine or an ensouled being?). Reality is perhaps not as easily comprehensible and accessible as a naive subject/object relationship might suggest. The natural context of cause and effect that is connected in an unusual or even new way, and God's promissory word that accounts for this connection must be seen together to perceive the whole of reality. This means that if we regard an event simply as a natural occurrence, this will lead to a truncation of the whole of reality. While the presence of God in any event, whether miraculous or not, is not scientifically demonstrable, seeing God and nature together brings the whole of reality into focus. This is also important for our consideration of the sacraments, since again natural elements (water, wine, bread, etc.) are used to convey divine grace.

NOTES

1. Walter Kaspar, "Law and Gospel," in *Sacramentum Mundi* 3:397.
2. Martin Luther, Lectures on Galatians (1519), *LW* 27:355, in his exegesis of Gal. 5:14.
3. Martin Luther, *WA* 49, 2, 1–2, in a sermon of 1 January 1540.
4. Karl Barth, "Gospel and Law," in *God, Grace, and Gospel*, trans. J. S. McNab (Edinburgh: Oliver & Boyd, 1959), 3.
5. Ibid., 8.
6. For this and the following quote, see ibid., 10.
7. Johann Wolfgang von Goethe, *Faust* II/V 7. 11936–37.
8. John Calvin, *Institutes of the Christian Religion* (2.7), ed. John T. McNeill, trans. F. L. Battles (Philadelphia: Westminster Press, 1960), 1:360.
9. Paul Althaus, *The Divine Command*, trans. F. Sherman, intro. William H. Lazareth. Facet Books (Philadelphia: Fortress Press, 1966).
10. *BC* 349.
11. For this and the following quote, see Martin Luther, Ninety-five Theses, *LW* 31:25.
12. Dietrich Bonhoeffer, *Letters and Papers from Prison*, rev. ed., ed. Eberhard Bethge, trans. R. Fuller (New York: Macmillan Co., 1967), 213.
13. Martin Luther, Sermon on the Gospel of St. John (1537), *LW* 24:81, in his exposition of John 14:12.
14. Augustine, *The City of God*, trans. M. Dods, intro. Thomas Merton (New York: Random House, 1950), 776 (21.8).
15. Rudolf Bultmann, "New Testament and Mythology," in *Kerygma and Myth. A Theological Debate*, ed. Hans-Werner Bartsch, trans. R. H. Fuller (London: SPCK, 1953). 5.

3

Baptism

The sacraments, celebrated at the command of the resurrected Christ and expressive of his salvific work, are the visible side of the pronouncement of God's redemptive word. Word and sacrament belong together as powerful instruments of God's grace. Christian baptism is the appropriation of Christ's death and resurrection by God, imparting the totality of salvation and grace to the one who is baptized. It is not merely an initiation rite into adulthood or full church membership. Confirmation is not an actual sacrament but primarily an act of personal commitment by which one publicly and actively acknowledges the divine sign of baptism. Infant baptism emphasizes the primacy of God's action and implies that the Christian community has an educational responsibility toward the baptized infant.

EXCURSUS: THE NATURE AND EFFICACY OF THE SACRAMENTS

Sacred rites are intrinsic to any religion, the Christian faith being no exception. The so-called rites of passage—beginning of life, initiation to adulthood, marriage, setting apart for divine service, penance, sacred meals, and the leaving this life—are celebrated in many different forms by virtually all religions. In considering the Christian sacraments, we could simply assume that they follow commonly established procedures. In some ways this may certainly be the case. Yet we should not forget that the central focus of all Christian sacraments is the life and destiny of Jesus of Nazareth.

Especially the churches of the Reformation emphasize the connection between the sacraments and Jesus Christ. The Heidelberg Catechism, for instance, states: "the Reformed Church recognizes only two sacraments; Baptism and the Lord's Supper, those which have been instituted by Jesus Christ."[1] Similarly, when Martin Luther introduces only two sacraments in his catechism, he refers to them as "instituted by Christ."[2] As soon as the historical connection between Jesus Christ and the sacraments is attenuated, the number of sacraments seems to become fluid. For instance, Philip Melanchthon arrives at three sacraments: baptism, the Lord's Supper, and absolution, when he defines the sacraments as "rites which have the command of God and to which the promise of grace has been added."[3] Yet, in contrast to the Roman Catholic Church and to the Reformed, Lutherans have never explicitly and unanimously stated a definite number of sacraments.

The Roman Catholic tradition perceives the sacraments much more as a function of the church. In *Sacramentum Mundi*, for example, which attempts to formulate prevailing considerations after Vatican II, we hear that the sacraments, "as defined in the theology of the Church, are the seven vital actions of the Church in its liturgy which are efficacious for salvation."[4] The sacraments are seen here much more as actions of the church instead of as actions on behalf of Christ. The sacraments are vital signs of the church. Certainly Lutherans would agree to this, when they say that the church "is the assembly of all believers among whom the Gospel is preached in its purity and the holy sacraments are administered according to the Gospel" (CA 7). Yet Protestants have traditionally considered vital functions of the church as sacraments only insofar as they, like the church itself, are instituted by Christ.

At this point, the Roman Catholic theologian Karl Rahner proposes a very interesting approach when he considers the church as "the final, irrevocable, eschatologically permanent word of salvation in the world" and, therefore, "the primary sacrament."[5] The argument now goes that since Christ instituted the church, he also instituted the sacraments which are not attested by any expressed text of Scripture. This mediated approach to the sacraments, being instituted by Christ through the church, allows for many more than the seven sacraments specified by present-day Catholicism. It also alleviates the necessity to ascertain in each instance that Jesus Christ, either as Jesus of history or as the resurrected Christ, did indeed institute a particular sacrament. But it also leaves us at the mercy of the church to recognize a particular action or rite as a sacrament since no criterion outside the church can be applied to discern a true sacrament from other rites. Much more serious is the conclusion that the sacraments would then be secondarily but not primarily related to Christ. Thus their intrinsic christocentric character would be dangerously attenuated.

The issue of what constitutes a true sacrament is further complicated by the fact that the term "sacrament" is not used in the Greek New Testament. The Latin term *sacramentum* initially had nothing to do with what we today understand by a sacrament. It could mean the sum of money that two parties to a law suit deposited. The sum deposited by the losing party was then used for religious purposes. It could also mean the military oath of allegiance. The latter use seems to have given rise to our theological understanding of the term "sacrament." The military connotations can still be seen in Tertullian when he says at the beginning of the third century: "We were called to the service in the army of the living God in the very moment when we gave response to the words of the sacramental oath."[6] Tertullian leaves no doubt that in performing the sacraments, we follow the command of the Lord. It is God who calls us and who asks for our response to his pledge of the sacrament. When we notice that God binds himself in the sacrament, inducing an obligation and a response from us, we must conclude that the judicial aspect of the sacrament is retained, too. We might not be wrong in assuming that the military and judicial roots of the term "sacrament" decidedly influenced the sacramental theology in the Western church. If God binds himself in the sacrament, then the question of the means of this oath had to emerge. For Christians it was obvious that God bound himself to the Christian community through his saving acts in Jesus Christ. Thus the christological component has always been central to the sacrament. Similarly, it was also obvious that God's oath would not be revoked. What was celebrated in the sacraments had enduring effect.

In the Latin Vulgate the term *sacramentum* is used to render the Greek *mysterion*. The term "mystery" is still used today in the Eastern tradition to denote the sacraments. In the New Testament, however, the term "mystery" does not refer to the sacraments, but primarily to the mystery of Christ (1 Cor. 2:1; Eph. 3:4) meaning the crucified, and to the secret (mystery) of the kingdom of God (Mark 4:11–12). The use of the term "mystery" for the sacraments invited the analogy to ancient mystery cults. These cults promised the devotees salvation and allowed them to participate in the suffering of the deity. The sacraments could then be understood as cultic rites in which the destiny of deity is portrayed in sacred action before the participants to make them part of that destiny. The church fathers were certainly aware of the danger in mixing the Christian sacraments with the pagan mystery cults, as we can see from Justin Martyr when he claims that "the wicked devils have imitated in the mysteries of Mithras" the celebration of the Eucharist, "commanding the same thing to be done."[7] Tertullian observes along the same line that the devil "by the mystic rites of his idols, vies even with the essential portions of the sacraments of God."[8] He also refers here to the Mithras cult, perhaps indicating its threatening nature to nascent Christianity and its affinity to its rituals.

Analogies to the mystery cults can also be found in the so-called arcanum discipline, especially prevalent in the Eastern church between the end of the second and the close of the fifth centuries. The idea was to keep secret the administration of baptism and Eucharist and related doctrines and rites from those who had not yet been initiated through baptism. In the fourth century John Chrysostom, for instance, says with reference to the Eucharist: "Those who partake of the mysteries understand what I say."[9] This emphasis on initiation and mystery puts the initiated into a different category from other people. Unlike the Latin sacrament with its military and judicial connotations, the Greek mystery implied a different state of being for the participant. Thus the quest for divinization and the emphasis on the incorporation into the redemptive drama reigned supreme.

The terms "sacrament" and "mystery" were initially used much more loosely than today. All kinds of sacred rituals and customs could be labeled sacraments, such as marriage, washing of the feet, anointing, ordination, confirmation, and, of course, baptism and Eucharist. When gradually a clearer notion emerged of what constitutes a sacrament, their number still varied considerably. For instance, Lafranc mentions four sacraments; Hugo of St. Victor seems to recognize five in his *Summa*, but in his treatise *On the Sacraments of the Christian Faith* he enumerates thirty including such religious customs as using holy water or ashes on Ash Wednesday. Since Peter Lombard the number was settled at seven, the same as in the Eastern church; and at the Council of Florence we hear: "There are seven sacraments of the New Law: namely baptism, confirmation, Eucharist, penance, extreme unction, orders and matrimony, which differ a great deal from the sacraments of the Old Law."[10] Settling on seven sacraments was facilitated by seven being a "sacred" number (cf. seven canonical hours, seven cardinal virtues, sevenfold orders of the clergy, etc.). The council stated also that "among these sacraments there are three, baptism, confirmation, and orders, which imprint an indelible sign on the soul, that is, a certain character distinctive from the others. Hence they should not be repeated in the same person."[11] From thereon the Roman Catholic tradition counted seven sacraments, three of which were not to be repeated since they left an indelible imprint. But even the others were not equal.

Very early baptism and Eucharist had a more prominent position than the other sacraments. Hugo of St. Victor even distinguished between three kinds of sacraments, those in which salvation primarily consists, those which either prepare or sanctify the things that are necessary for the sanctification and institution of the other sacraments, and those which, while not necessary for salvation, contribute to sanctification.[12] Yet in some ways all the sacraments have similar features. They are administered by the priest; they connect God's word with a sign and thereby affect the soul. Sacraments are visible signs of the invisible grace.

Since for Christians grace is intimately connected with Christ's salvific work, the sacraments are expressive of Christ's salvific word. For instance, in baptism the dying and rising with Christ is central; and in the Eucharist, the participation in Christ's body and blood is central. When Augustine claims here that the sacraments "contain the announcement that He [Christ] has been born, has suffered, has risen," then this definition could hardly be adduced to substantiate all seven sacraments.[13] For him, a sacrament is intimately connected with the gospel of Christ: "the word is added to the element, and there results the Sacrament, as if itself also a kind of visible word."[14] Concerning baptism, for instance, Augustine stated: "Take away the word, and the water is neither more nor less than water." Martin Luther echoed the same sentiments a thousand years later when he wrote in his Small Catechism: "It is not the water that produces these effects, but the Word of God connected with the water, and our faith which relies on the Word of God connected with the water."[15]

Sacraments are the visible side of the pronouncement of God's redemptive word. They depict the invisible grace that is announced and administered in them, and their elements bear a semblance of that salvation history which they signify. Since they are not magic rituals, the elements need not be slavishly followed (e.g., in an emergency one can also baptize with sand, or substitute grape juice for wine) but there should be some resemblance to that which is depicted. The signs do not point to an eternal truth or to magic rituals but to God's history in Jesus Christ. To underscore the distinction between sign and the signifying action, medieval theology rightly distinguished between *materia* ("elements used") or *sacramentum* and *forma* or *res sacramenti* ("the spiritual or invisible grace") in considering the sacraments as the visible form of the invisible grace (so Hugo of St. Victor).

Since the sacraments are the visible side of God's redemptive word, their efficacy is analogous to that of the word. Neither word nor sacrament is higher in rank. The Augsburg Confession affirmed the sameness of their efficacy when it said: "Through the Word and the sacraments, as through instruments, the Holy Spirit is given, and the Holy Spirit produces faith, where and when it pleases God, in those who hear the Gospel" (CA 5).

Since the sacraments are powerful instruments of God's grace and not human rites, their efficacy does not depend on the spiritual state of those who administer them. Of course, the sacraments should not be administered casually but in compliance with their stated promise. In most cases it would be nearly impossible to ascertain with sufficient certainty the spiritual worthiness of the celebrant. A reflection on the celebrant might also induce the idea that the sacraments are dependent on the celebrant rather than him or her being a medium or vehicle of God's grace. The Augsburg Confession picked up this issue when it asserted: "Both the sacraments and the Word are effectual by reason of the institution and commandment of Christ even if they are administered by evil men" (CA 8). Since the celebrant can neither further nor hinder the efficacy of the sacraments, sacraments administered by heretics can also be accepted as valid. Ministers should always be examples of faith and conduct, however, so as not to detract the faithful but to inspire them in the proper use of the sacraments.

If the sacraments can be effective irrespective of the worthiness of the celebrant, the question must be asked whether any precondition on the side of the recipient is necessary to assure efficacy. Two assertions at the Council of Trent have especially caused much dissatisfaction among Protestants. The council declared that the sacraments confer grace "on those who do not place an obstacle in the way," implying the notion of cooperation toward salvation.[16] The council also stated that in the sacraments grace is "conferred from the work which has been worked," which usually has been interpreted to mean that the gift is automatically conferred through that which has been accomplished.[17] But today Roman Catholic scholars do not admit that this would imply an automatic or mechanical way in which the sacraments produce their effects or some sort of magic. Similar to Protestants, the Roman Catholics want to express through the phrase "from the work which has been worked [*ex opere operato*]" that the mediation of grace is not dependent on the personal merits of the participant or the celebrant of the sacraments. Karl Rahner even affirms: "The *opus operatum* is the eschatologically efficacious word of God."[18] God sees to it that his word will not return empty but delivers the promises contained in it.

The other issue that needs further investigation is the idea of cooperation. When we hear today that "the mediation of grace, both in its actual occurrence and in its 'measure' is essentially dependent on the disposition of the recipient," our fears are not alleviated.[19] Yet Protestants are not very far from this position. Though most Lutherans usually hesitate to admit it, even the Augsburg Confession does not totally exclude reflection upon the condition of the recipient when it says that "the Holy Spirit produces faith . . . in those who hear the Gospel" (CA 5). Similarly Martin Luther states in the Small Catechism that "the Word of God connected with the water, and our faith which relies on the Word of God connected with the water" produces these great saving effects.[20]

In the light of these statements even Lutherans are not relegated to passivity, letting God do everything. If that were so, Lutherans could not avoid a mechanistic understanding of the mediation of divine grace or a kind of predestination through which we are the victim rather than the sought-after lost sheep. Yet we wonder whether the Roman Catholic side has not overemphasized the necessary reflection on the recipients and their disposition when we hear that the mediation of grace "depends on the faith of the recipient as he lays himself open and surrenders to the sacramental grace, as also on the intention of the recipient."[21] It is indeed important to emphasize the necessity for openness. But if a human being in its sinfulness is turned in on itself, how can such openness be properly achieved?

Most recent discussions between Roman Catholics and Lutherans have gone beyond the position just mentioned which initially resulted from Vatican II. Now we hear that "according to Catholic doctrine the *ex opere operato* should witness in the context of the sacramentology to the priority of God's action. To stress this priority is likewise the concern of the Lutherans."[22] What the Roman Catholic doctrine expresses by the statement about the effectiveness of the sacraments *ex opere operato* is in its essence Lutheran teaching too: God's offer of grace does not stand or fall with the faith or the unbelief of the recipient nor does it depend on the worthiness of the one officiating.

Before we turn to the discussion of specific sacraments, we must briefly ask what kind of grace is conveyed in the sacraments and whether the sacraments offer something not attainable through the spoken word. Again Trent may baffle us when it states that through the sacraments of the church "all true justice either begins, or being begun is increased, or being lost is restored."[23] Would this mean that the word is only preparation for the reception of justification, while true justification occurs through the acceptance of the sacraments? Truly, Trent rejects the idea that "without them or without the desire of them through faith alone men obtain from God the grace of justification." But Trent distinguishes between the reception of the sacraments and the desire to receive them. It states that either one is acceptable since in some extreme situations the sacraments may be unavailable while the desire to receive them persists. Yet, Trent affirms that a flat rejection of the sacraments would not lead to salvation. Similarly, Lutherans would say that whoever flatly rejects the sacraments has at the most a truncated understanding of the word as God's self-disclosive action, since the sacraments are the visible aspect of this action. This would then mean that both Roman Catholics and Lutherans do not want to elevate the sacraments above the spoken (preached) word but see them in line with it.

The question still needs attention why the reception of the sacraments and justification are so closely, if not exclusively, connected. Does this not imply a devaluation of the significance of preached word? Indeed, word and sacrament are inseparable in that both offer and convey to us God's grace. Nevertheless, we talk about baptismal grace, the grace conveyed through ordination, and the grace obtained through penance. While this does not mean that there are different graces, there are certainly different aspects to it. But there is no ascent from the mere encounter with preached word to the participation in the sacraments. On the other hand, an encounter with the word that does not lead to participation in the sacraments is not a full encounter with God. While the power of the gospel suffices for salvation (Rom. 1:16), the gospel is not confined to the word but includes both word and sacrament. Both word and sacrament work together toward salvation. When the Council of Trent turned its attention to the sacraments, it fittingly emphasized their salvational quality. We might, of course, wonder why at Trent a similar emphasis is not placed on the word. But if we want to look for a Roman Catholic emphasis on the word, we should not look to Trent, a document of the Counter-Reformation, but to Vatican II, a document which introduced a truly evangelical tone.

But Lutherans are really not unanimous in asserting the essential equality of word and sacrament. For instance, Philip Melanchthon wrote with reference to Augustine in his Apology of the Augsburg Confession that "the Word and the rite have the same effect."[24] Most of the classical dogmaticians advanced this interpretation. But we should not collapse word and sacrament into each other. Though having the same effect, they are not identical. Some Lutherans, especially in the nineteenth century, went beyond this distinction and also attempted to ascertain a difference in effect. This attempt to assert a greater significance for one of them was mostly connected with the Lord's Supper. It was claimed that there ought to be a difference through divine self-mediation between our encounter with the word alone and our encounter with the elements of wine and bread. For instance, one thought that the spoken word addresses the inner person, while the sacrament addresses the physical side of humanity. Gottfried Thomasius of the Erlangen School taught that the "word mediated communion with the spirit of Christ, so that total salvation pertains to the whole of humanity and the whole person is saved and sanctified."[25] Some even thought of the elements as nourishment for the future new body. We will encounter these thoughts again when we investigate the Greek notion of deification.

Although it is difficult to assert that the word could have an effect other than that of the sacraments, we must note that each leaves a different impression. While the word is usually addressed to everybody who can hear, the sacraments always single out one person, conveying God's grace to a specific person. A sermon (preached word) could convey the impression, albeit wrongly, that we encounter only the word of the proclaimer instead of God's word, or that God's word does not pertain to us. But when through the sacraments God's grace is conveyed to a specific person, no uncertainty should remain. The person is singled out as the recipient of God's grace. Since the conveyance of God's grace in the sacraments does not address just one of the senses, hearing, but sight, smell, taste, and touch as well, a much wider appeal to the person is possible than with the spoken word alone. The whole person with all its senses is drawn into salvation history. Yet we dare not forget that the word makes all the difference. Without it, the sacrament would remain an empty sign. The word is not just a part of the sacrament but the essential part, while all the other items are signaling that to which the word points. Perhaps because of the total involvement of the person, the sacraments are more attractive—as indicated by better worship attendance on Sundays celebrating Holy Communion—than a mere service of the word. The tendency in Protestant churches toward a more frequent offering of the sacraments perhaps underscores this factor. Since the celebration of the sacraments is never without the interpretive and specifying word, such moves would not devaluate the word but show it in its essential correlation with the sacrament. Conversely, we encounter services of the word more regularly now in Roman Catholic churches. This would underscore the understanding that the Eucharist is not the only means of God's self-disclosive action. He conveys his grace to us also through the spoken (preached) word.

THE BIBLICAL FOUNDATION OF BAPTISM

The New Testament tells us that the institution of the Christian baptism dates back to a command of the resurrected Christ but not to the Jesus of history (Matt. 28:19; Mark 16:16). But the practice of baptism certainly cannot be divorced from the life of Jesus. The

Synoptics report that Jesus himself was baptized (Mark 1:9–11 par.), and we infer that John the Baptist baptized Jesus through God's authority (Mark 11:27–33). While the Gospel of John mentions that Jesus himself occasionally baptized (John 3:22; 4:1), John 4:2 denies that. But why should the Christian community develop a Christian baptismal practice if such a custom did not originate with Jesus of Nazareth? A partial answer may be given when we hear that the resurrected Christ introduces baptism as a necessary precondition for salvation when he states: "He who believes and is baptized will be saved" (Mark 16:16). The same is implied when the Gospel of John tells us that Jesus addressed Nicodemus: "Unless one is born of water and the Spirit, he cannot enter the kingdom of God" (John 3:5). Furthermore, most religious groups have certain initiation rites, and the Christian community is no exception.

Turning to Paul, we observe that baptism is not just an initiation rite by which we enter a special community. He says: "We were buried therefore with him by baptism into death, so that as Christ was raised from the dead by the glory of the Father, we too might walk in newness of life" (Rom. 6:4). Since the Christian baptism is the appropriation of Jesus' death and resurrection, it cannot date back to Jesus of Nazareth. Only the resurrected one could give the command to baptize. Baptism does not just initiate into a certain community, it makes one participate in the salvational benefits of Jesus Christ. In this light the saying of Jesus, "If any man would come after me, let him deny himself and take up his cross and follow me" (Mark 8:34), takes a new meaning. To become a follower of Jesus means to renounce the former life, to take over his salvational benefits through baptism and to become a new being. The baptized one receives Christ's salvific benefits and becomes his property.

While Jesus affirmed the baptism of John the Baptist, the Christian baptism cannot be seen simply in analogy to John's baptism of repentance. The Christian baptism has eschatological significance as indicated already in John's prediction: "I baptize you with water for repentance, but he who is coming after me . . . will baptize you with the Holy Spirit and with fire" (Matt. 3:11). A baptism in Christ does entail the Holy Spirit and leads beyond the metaphoric fire of judgment. In other words, it leads to new life. John's baptism by water is not replaced through a baptism by the Spirit but both are connected to the Christian baptism in the name of Jesus. It is interesting in this context that Paul, coming to Ephesus, finds a group of people who were baptized by John the Baptist but did not have the Holy Spirit (Acts 19:1–7). As soon as they were baptized in the name of Jesus Christ and Paul had laid his hands upon them, they received the Holy Spirit. Occasionally, there even seems to be a distinction made between the actual baptism (for repentance) and the laying on of hands (imparting the Spirit) (Acts 8:12, 14–19; Acts 10:44–48). But both are so closely connected with each other that we cannot speak of separate rites.[26] The eschatological gift, the Spirit, is imparted through baptism and leads to new life.

As soon as the Holy Spirit was poured out on the apostles at Pentecost, they began to baptize. From thereon baptism was a regular activity of the missionary endeavor of the Christian community. One of the first prominent Jews to be baptized was Paul. After he had encountered Christ on the road to Damascus, he was baptized and received the Holy Spirit (Acts 9:17–18). While Paul did not start the Christian practice of baptizing converts (Rom. 6:3), he decidedly influenced the Christian understanding of baptism. Most revealing is chapter 6 in his Letter to the Romans in which he uses terminology prevalent in Hellenistic communities when he talks about the dying and rising of the baptized one with Christ.[27]

In the mystery cults, such as the cult of Mithras popular in the Roman Empire, the idea of death and rebirth of the one to be initiated played an important role. Often there were periods of purification and preparation preceding the actual initiation, and there is frequent reference to ablutions. The initiation ceremonies usually mimed death and resurrection. Often this was done in a rather dramatic manner. For instance, the candidates could be buried or shut up in a sarcophagus, they could be symbolically deprived of their entrails and mummified, or even symbolically drowned or decapitated. The intention of these rituals was clear—to indicate a complete break with the former ways and the beginning of a totally new life. The latter was often symbolized through the giving of a new name. In mystery religions, the destiny of the godhead, death and resurrection, was usually understood as being transferable to the believer.

Paul comes close to these ideas in showing that our baptism enables us to participate in Christ's death and resurrection. Yet he does not talk about initiation or consecration as would be expected in mystery religions. There is also no mention of a divine myth or a cycle of death and rebirth of the godhead or the initiate as would be normal for mystery religions. It is characteristic for Paul and the Christian message that he relates the dying and rising of the baptized to the singular and unique historical event of Christ's death and resurrection. Through the reality symbolized by water baptism we are cleansed from our sins. We are made participants in the benefits of Christ's death and resurrection; and we are certain of our own life, which to some extent we already enjoy, and of the future resurrection. Contrary to the mystery cults, we should not shroud our experience of new life in silence, but Paul encourages us to show forth this new creation in daily living (Rom. 6:4). The fact of our new existence of freedom should lead to the living out of its consequences.

Paul was not confined to one particular set of conceptual tools to talk about baptism. Among others, he would use mystery imagery, ontological terminology, or even juridical terms. For instance, he says with reference to our new state of being: "For as many of you as were baptized into Christ have put on Christ" (Gal. 3:27), indicating the transfer of Christ's destiny. Or, "Therefore, if any one is in Christ, he is a new creation" (2 Cor. 5:17), connecting baptism with creation and employing ontological concepts. He also mentions that God has put his seal upon us so we are his property and has given us his Spirit in our hearts as a guarantee (2 Cor. 1:21–22). From Paul's argument in 2 Cor. 1:21–22 it becomes obvious that there is a fine line between mere symbolism and magical action.[28] There is an eschatological reality to the baptismal action, since we have the guarantee, or rather down payment, of the Holy Spirit. This *arrabon* ("down payment") is a juridical term. It does not mean that only the initial down payment of the Spirit is given and further installments of the Spirit will follow. Rather the Spirit is a down payment for something. The something is not mentioned but was evident for the readers. It could only mean the eschatological salvation and the full inheritance as children of God (cf. Eph. 1:14).

There is yet another juridical term which Paul uses in connection with baptism, namely *bebaion* ("to establish or to make strong"). Not in a magical way but in an "objective" way the newly baptized is made part of Christ. Paul even becomes more explicit when he mentions that we are anointed (*chrisas*). Though an anointing of the baptized with oil can at best be ascertained for the postapostolic time, Paul uses this metaphorical term to show that the baptized is for all intents and purposes anointed and joins thereby into communion with the anointed one, the Messiah. The baptized is made part of the messianic community which in Paul's time was virtually identical with the Christian community. Since Paul talks about baptizing (with water) as an anointing, he practically excludes the possibility of complete immersion.

Finally we notice that Paul mentions the putting upon us of his seal. Again the juridical component is obvious. We are marked with the seal "for the day of redemption" (Eph. 4:30). We become Christ's property and are marked for the day of judgment enjoying his protection in and through judgment. Whether the seal is meant to be the sign of the cross is not certain. The practice of sealing with the sign of the cross is not attested until the postapostolic period. Yet Paul certainly wanted to assure the people in Corinth that baptism is more than magic or symbolism. It results in the juridically unwavering conviction of our new being in Christ. A Christian is a new person, not just on the psychological level—there often the least—but in reality, before and in Christ.

But baptism does not automatically save us. Though we cannot undo it, it is always possible to break away from the covenant that God establishes with us in baptism (cf. 1 Cor. 10:1–5). Since baptism is administered within the Christian community, it should not be perceived as an individualistic act occurring only between Christ and us. Being incorporated into the body of Christ, we are all one (Gal. 3:28); and Christ's Spirit intensifies the unifying function of baptism (1 Cor. 12:12). Since baptism also means incorporation into the visible body of Christ, it establishes the unity between Christians and makes us members of the body of Christ in terms of the visible and the celestial church. This corporate dimension of baptism has its analogies in the Jewish baptism of proselytes. When pagans converted to Judaism, they were baptized together with their children. If children were born after their parents had been baptized, they did not need to be baptized since they had become members of the Jewish community through their parents.

We find a very peculiar situation in the New Testament with

regard to the Christian baptismal practice. While the time span covered would have allowed for baptisms of second-generation Christians, the New Testament is silent on the baptism of descendants of Christians, whether infants or adults. We might be initially inclined to assume that the reason for this was the affinity to Jewish proselyte baptism. Christian baptism would then be only applicable to those who entered the Christian community from outside but not to those who were born within it. Paul even tells the Christians in Corinth that "the unbelieving husband is consecrated through his wife, and the unbelieving wife is consecrated through her husband. Otherwise, your children would be unclean, but as it is they are holy" (1 Cor. 7:14). But exegetes tell us that this passage does not speak to our issue and that we should not conclude from this statement that a child sanctified through its parents need not be baptized.[29] Paul does not address here the issue of baptism, but simply states that, in dealing with non-Christian members of a Christian family, we are confronted with people who are already in the Christian sphere and not with those who are under the influence of foreign or demonic powers. If infants are already within the Christian sphere of influence, we should expect that this affiliation with the Christian faith is formalized and officially sanctioned. This means that though it is nowhere expressly stated in the New Testament, infants of Christians should also be baptized. Similar to the baptismal imagery indicating parallels to the mystery cults, the analogy to proselyte baptism does not do justice to the whole Christian understanding of baptism. Furthermore, there is the analogy of circumcision to baptism (Col. 2:11–12), which would certainly imply that infants born within the fold of faith would be baptized, as they have been circumcised in Israel.

THE MEANING OF BAPTISM FOR TODAY

A theological assessment of the Christian baptism cannot, however, begin with infant baptism. It must start with the initial and original practice of baptism in the context of mission and conversion. Baptism is first of all something which occurs with someone and which that person wants to have performed. It is not done by force, against the will of a person, but voluntarily. The active and passive moods come together in baptism. For the one who is being baptized, baptism is the sign and seal of repentance and affirmation of faith. Thus, baptism and oral confession of faith belong together. For instance, when people came to John the Baptist, they confessed their sins (Mark 1:5). Similarly, Christian baptism has always been connected with the confession of sins, professing that Jesus Christ is Lord, and calling on his name (Acts 22:16). The one who wants to be baptized asks for baptism and comes to it. The formula *ti kolyei* ("what prevents me"), which occurs frequently in connection with conversion baptisms (cf. Acts 8:36), has juridical connotations and presupposes some kind of examination about possible hindrances to baptism. An insert in part of the Western textual tradition in the story of the baptism of the minister of Candace points in the same direction. After the minister asked: "What is to prevent my being baptized?" (Acts 8:37), the text continues: "If you believe with all your heart, you may (be baptized)" and the response: "I believe that Jesus Christ is the Son of God." A credal confession in Jesus as the Lord (cf. Rom. 10:9) is a necessary part of baptism.

Decisive for our understanding of baptism today is what happens to the candidates. Baptism is neither an act of the candidates nor of the one who administers it. Since the middle of the second century baptism is administered in the name of the triune God.[30] Because of Christ's death and resurrection, baptism is an act of God. Through baptism the baptized will be given over to the triune God who receives them in grace and calls them into communion (1 Cor. 1:9). This dedication to Christ, the reception into fellowship with God, is underscored through the outward ritual. What occurs at baptism must be seen in analogy to the Old Testament "prophetic symbolism where the action and the meaning are one."[31] Through the water the body is washed and cleansed of all impurities (sins). God forgives the baptized for all sins and pronounces them justified and holy (1 Cor. 6:11). In the original rite of immersion, death of the old Adam and resurrection to new life were depicted even more drastically. Through baptism the death penalty that is pronounced over all people is actualized. But at the same time, through Christ's death and resurrection, there is the demonstration of new life.

In baptism we receive God's grace and are made part of the New Covenant. This means that salvation and grace in its totality are imparted to us at baptism. We are full members of the body of Christ and not initiates that have just passed the first of several exams. Similarly, the effect of baptism is the conveyance of God's full grace. It opens for us communion with God. Thus it is understandable that the question has been raised whether baptism should not immediately lead to the Eucharist or whether the proper place for baptism is not the eucharistic service. While the second part of the question can easily be answered in the affirmative, the first part needs more detailed discussion as we will see later.

The grace that God extends to us in baptism is not contingent upon our faith. We must remember here the statement of Augustine that grace is not grace unless it is gratis. If it were contingent upon us, baptism could only be effective if we agreed to it. Yet God accepts us before we accept him, similar to him sending Jesus to us before we believe in Jesus as the Christ. But if we reject God's offer, if we do not respond to his unconditionally given grace, it simply lays dormant. There is no magic involved in baptism that would do something with us regardless of what we did. God's prevenient grace necessitates our response to make baptism into an instrument of his saving grace. Since baptism is constituted by God's unique offer of acceptance and not by our wavering spirit, there is no need to repeat baptism if we return to him. We can deny God's grace, but we cannot lose it. We are always children of God, regardless how we behave. Thus there is no need to repeat the baptismal convenant, but to grasp it anew. In his Large Catechism Martin Luther, using St. Jerome's metaphor, very appropriately compared baptism with a boat:

> Baptism remains forever. Even though we fall from it and sin, nevertheless we always have access to it so that we may again subdue the old man. But we need not again have the water poured over us. Even if we were immersed in water a hundred times, it would nevertheless be only one Baptism, and the effect and signification of Baptism would continue and remain. Repentance, therefore, is nothing else than a return and approach to Baptism, to resume and practice what had earlier been begun but abandoned. . . . The ship does not founder, since, as we said, it is God's ordinance and not a word of ours. But

it does happen that we slip and fall out of the ship. If anybody does fall out, he should immediately head for the ship and cling to it until he can climb aboard again and sail on it as he had done before.[32]

In baptism God extends his hand to save us. The question put to us is whether we grasp it. While the affirmative part at baptism is important it is always subsequent to God's initiative, but not constitutive for it. The acceptance God expresses toward us at baptism is then to be actualized throughout a lifetime. "The old Adam in us, together with all sins and evil lusts, should be drowned by daily sorrow and repentance and be put to death," as Luther reminds us in this Small Catechism.[33] The Christian life is nothing but a daily baptism through which we continuously affirm what God has done to us so that the new person "should come forth daily and rise up, cleansed and righteous, to live forever in God's presence."

The existential actualization of baptism, emphasized by Luther, would remain an empty phrase without its underlying juridical and eschatological significance. Baptism denotes not only a change of allegiance, from the allegiance to the world to that of God, but a change in belonging. A child of this world and its sinfulness becomes a child of God and his promises. The naming of the baptized one in the baptismal rite indicates that she or he has become a different person. In the missionary context, for instance, the old pagan name is put aside and a new Christian name is assumed. Similarly, in infant baptism the nameless baby is now given a Christian name. That the Christian name often reflects so little of our Christian faith may be indicative of how little we realize that listening to a different tune (name) expresses a different sense of belonging. In baptism we become fully and really children of God.

By becoming children of God, that is, his daughters and sons, we become full members of his kingdom, with all rights, privileges, and duties pertaining to it. The occasional idea that there is a baptism by the Holy Spirit which is separate from the baptism by water would imply that water baptism is only a symbolic act—though this opinion usually leaves us in the dark as to what it should be symbolic of—while a later baptism by the Holy Spirit is the real activity of God. At this later act the gifts of the Spirit, of which speaking in tongues is often understood to be primary, are bestowed upon the baptized one. Three points should be remembered in the context of this issue: (1) Through baptism we become full members of God's kingdom, that is, his property. There is no associate membership possible. It is either full or none. (2) "The external rite of water-purification cannot be separated or divorced from the inner rite of soul-purification."[34] Action and meaning are one and interpret one another. (3) Baptism in the name of the triune God, Father, Son, and Holy Spirit, makes it clear that Christ and the Spirit cannot be separated or divorced. "Any one who does not have the Spirit of Christ does not belong to him," says Paul (Rom. 8:9). And "now the Lord is the Spirit," he tells the Christians in Corinth (2 Cor. 3:17). Through baptism the Christian becomes a new creation. She or he obtains all the gifts the Spirit will ever pour out on us, including the promise of new life (cf. also Acts 2:38 and Titus 3:5).

Being endowed with the Holy Spirit reminds us, however, that the Spirit is an eschatological gift. Essentially it is a witness and a down payment of something to come, the disclosure of the fullness of the kingdom. Thus the eschatological dimension, its proviso character, its proleptic anticipation, and its expectant longing, dare not be forgotten. Otherwise baptism remains a sacrament of this world and a symbol that one gets what one sees. Rather baptism opens for us the larger dimension of the kingdom; we become heirs in hope of eternal life. Baptism joins us together with all the company of heaven, with Christians past, present, and future. The body of Christ in which we are implanted through baptism is larger than any denomination, even all denominations taken together.

Yet baptism also means incorporation into the visible church. Similar to the sacraments, the church too has a visible dimension. While a Christian can never just be a member of a local congregation unless she or he would denigrate this local manifestation of the church to a social club, one can never be a Christian without belonging to a local congregation. Baptism and local membership go together. In contrast to a marriage ceremony, baptism is always a rite which takes place within the context of a particular congregation. Thus the baptismal certificate is issued by the pastor of a local congregation or his or her representative. Within the local congregation, but not confined to it, is the arena in which the baptized ones bear witness to their new qualities as children of God. That some qualities (gifts) are more emphasized than others and that some may even lay dormant for a while may reflect the needs of the community as much as the special tasks and opportunities of the individual.

Finally, we must reflect on the relationship of faith and baptism. "He who believes and is baptized will be saved" we read in an appendix to Mark's Gospel (16:16). Yet faith is not something that we bring to baptism as a precondition. Paul reminds us: "So faith comes from what is heard, and what is heard comes by the preaching of Christ" (Rom. 10:17). Not by accident do homilies for baptismal instruction rank among the earliest extant Christian literature. Of course, one could say that at one point our decision to believe must be made and the desire to be baptized be expressed. Yet the story of Philip and the minister of Queen Candace is very instructive at this point. When Philip asked: "Do you understand what you are reading?" the minister replied: "How can I, unless some one guides me?" (Acts 8:30–31). We do not decide on our own to have faith. Someone always instructs us in faith.

Thus the passive mode of being offered the good news always precedes the active mode of acceptance. But the acceptance too, as Luther reminds us, is ultimately not self-wrought; it is a gift of God. So Luther comments in his explanation of the third article of the Apostles' Creed: "I believe that by my own reason or strength I cannot believe in Jesus Christ, my Lord, or come to him. But the Holy Spirit has called me through the Gospel, enlightens me with his gifts . . . in one true faith."[35] Faith belongs to baptism in an antecedent, concomitant, and subsequent way. In the confession of faith it precedes baptism. In the act of faith it relies on the promise of God connected with water baptism. In a thrust of faith it participates in the hope founded on baptism. In the fourth century Basil the Great expressed the relationship between faith and baptism best when he said:

> Faith and baptism are two kindred and inseparable ways of salvation: faith is perfected through baptism, baptism through faith, and both are completed by the same names. For as we believe in the Father and the

> Son and the Holy Ghost, so are we also baptized in the name of the Father and of the Son and of the Holy Ghost; first comes the confession, introducing us to salvation, and baptism follows, setting the seal upon our assent.[36]

Complete as baptism is, there seems to be another step that brings to completion that which has started in baptism. This is, at least, a frequent understanding of the rite of confirmation, a notion which deems further investigation.

THE SIGNIFICANCE OF CONFIRMATION

Representative of many Roman Catholic theologians, Michael Schmaus in his *Der Glaube der Kirche (The Faith of the Church)* concedes that it took a long time for confirmation to be clearly recognized as a sacrament in its own right which was distinct from baptism.[37] Together with baptism, he asserts, it forms the complete rite of initiation. Yet Schmaus does not want to distinguish both in such a way that one is initiated at baptism into Christ and into the Holy Spirit at confirmation. As all sacraments, baptism and confirmation are signs of Easter and Pentecost.

Schmaus also concedes that the adoption of confirmation as a sacrament resulted from a free decision of the church. We remember that in the early church after baptism there often occurred the laying on of hands and anointing. Though it is not always clear whether this act still belonged to the rite of baptism or was considered an independent act of confirmation, Schmaus assumes the latter. Gradually the rite of anointing was separated more and more from the rite of baptism and also replaced the laying on of hands.[38] By the middle of the third century this rite was generally accepted in the West. Baptism then attained a more negative aspect (cleansing from sin), while anointing was seen as having a more positive aspect (imparting the gift of the Holy Spirit). Since the Holy Spirit is given through baptism too, it was thought to be completed through anointing. In baptism a weakness in the newborn still persists that is then alleviated through another sacrament.

As more and more people joined the church after the Christian faith had become the official religion under Emperor Constantine, the dioceses became too large and were divided in smaller parishes. There the presbyters conducted baptisms on their own while the bishop alone anointed and sealed the baptized ones with the sign of the cross. But this confirmation by the bishop, the term "confirmation" is first mentioned in 411 at the Council of Orange, is conducted immediately after baptism. Since confirmation was administered by the bishop in the West, popular piety often regarded it higher than baptism for which the priest sufficed.

In the East the anointing (called chrismation and not confirmation) has usually been conducted by the priest immediately following baptism. But the oil used for the rite was consecrated before by the bishop. Regardless of this difference in practice that persists until today, the Eastern chrismation is accepted as valid confirmation by the West.

In the West confirmation was gradually separated by time from baptism, especially since the twelfth century when it was considered the precondition for participating in Eucharist. In the thirteenth century it was usually the seven-year-old child who received confirmation and subsequent communion. In the *Roman Catechism* (1566) the age was raised to twelve, while at present it has been lowered again.

In 1439 at the Council of Florence the church officially recognized confirmation "as the second sacrament" (after baptism). It was performed by the bishop with chrism, which he himself had consecrated.[39] In special cases the Holy See also gave priests the permission to administer confirmation. The effect of confirmation was understood to be the imparting of the Holy Spirit through which the confirmed youths would be strengthened so that they might valiantly confess their faith. Over against the Reformers, who insisted that confirmation was not a sacrament, the Roman Catholic Church emphasized even more its sacramental character. The Council of Trent declared that confirmation is "a true and proper sacrament" which the bishop alone can administer.[40]

Centuries later, Vatican II introduced several significant new aspects. It decreed that the rite of confirmation was to be revised and that "the intimate connection which this sacrament has with the whole of Christian initiation is to be more lucidly set forth."[41] This means it should be more closely related to baptism, theologically at least. That the council wanted to return to earlier practices also became evident when it said: "This sacred Ecumenical Synod endorses and lauds the ancient discipline of the sacraments existing in the eastern Churches. . . . With respect to the minister of holy chrism (confirmation), let that practice be fully restored which existed among Easterners in most ancient times. Priests, therefore, can validly confer this sacrament, provided they use chrism blessed by a Patriarch or a bishop."[42] Priests of the Eastern rite can administer confirmation validly in their churches. Even Latin priests can administer this sacrament to the faithful from the Eastern rite. Yet is the closer connection with baptism and the possibility of the priest administering confirmation sufficient to alleviate the criticism of the Reformers?

Martin Luther attacked the sacramental status of confirmation in the Babylonian Captivity of the Church (1520), preferring to call it a rite of which there are many others in the church. He wished that the church would return to the laying on of hands that prevailed at the time of the apostles. In a sermon on 15 March 1523 Luther suggested: "Confirmation should not be observed as the bishops desire it. Nevertheless we do not find fault if every pastor examines the faith of the children to see whether it is good and sincere, lays hands on them, and confirms them."[43] Luther implied that he tolerated confirmation if it consisted in a solemn blessing of the children who had previously been instructed in the faith. This rite would then also allow them to assume adult membership in the church and to participate in the Eucharist. Though this is virtually the way confirmation is understood and administered today in most Lutheran churches, he left it to others to devise an actual order of confirmation.

John Calvin also attacked the sacramental status of confirmation with the comment "that this pretended sacrament is nowhere recommended in scripture, either under this name or with this ritual, or this signification."[44] Furthermore, confirmation detracts from baptism. Similar to most Reformers, Calvin thought that there was a pure form of confirmation in the ancient church, before it was distorted to the Roman abuse of his time. He wanted to have this ancient custom restored in its pure form as "a catechetical exercise, in which children or youth used to deliver an account of their faith in the presence of the church."[45] Yet he too did not develop an order of confirmation.

Ulrich Zwingli also denied that confirmation was a sacrament and believed that it had its origin when it became common for infants to be baptized,[46] thus serving as some kind of catechumenate for the baptized infants. Though this assumption has no basis in history, in some way or other it provided the ground for the Protestant rite of confirmation.

Martin Bucer, Reformer at Strassburg, is often called the father of the Protestant rite of confirmation. He published an order of confirmation for the city of Strassburg (1534), though we are not sure whether he was able to put it into practice there. Nevertheless, upon invitation of the Landgrave Philip of Hesse he was able to actualize one in Ziegenhain and Kassel (1538/39).[47] Bucer found the peace of the church in Strassburg severely disturbed through the presence of Anabaptists and followers of Caspar Schwenkfeld. He countered their charge of moral laxity against the church which allowed infants to be baptized by designing an order of public confession of faith connected with laying on of hands and prayer. This rite would take place about the same age when the children of the Anabaptists confessed their faith and received baptism. Such a rite, which presupposed that the children had catechetical instruction, was intended to be offered twice a year, in the spring and in the fall. At the conclusion of this rite the children together with their sponsors and parents were admitted to the Lord's Table. In many other churches this "purified" confirmation found easy access. In Geneva, for instance, four times a year, before the Sundays on which the Eucharist was celebrated, such initiation of ten-year-old youths into the eucharistic community took place. Yet there the main emphasis of confirmation was to prepare for admission to the Lord's Table. Bucer's own order, however, picks up with baptism (repetition of the baptismal confession) and leads over to the Eucharist.

If infant baptism is practiced, it is indeed good and thoughtful to make explicit the implicit dedication to Christ that occurred in baptism and also the reception of God's grace. Confirmation primarily as an act of personal commitment by which we publicly and actively acknowledge the divine sign of baptism, does not devaluate or compromise baptism. Yet if confirmation is considered a sacramental completion of baptism and separated in time from the latter, baptism cannot remain a complete sacrament. This is still largely the position of the Roman Catholic Church where we hear that confirmation "as sacrament of consecration in Christian initiation, perfects baptism and is the normal preparation for the full ecclesial communion in the Eucharist."[48] So there are three essential elements: consecration, perfection of baptism, and preparation for the Eucharist. While we have little trouble acknowledging the validity of the first point and could also concede the third, a perfection of baptism unduly devaluates this fundamental sacrament.

The question must also be raised whether there can be different graces, as a sacramental understanding of confirmation suggests, or only different aspects of the same grace. If confirmation is the completion of the initiation rite, then we should assume that until confirmation is performed, one is not yet a full member of the body of Christ. Such thought would invalidate the whole notion of the baptismal covenant which is extended. But a confirmation rite certainly has merit. As a sacrament, however, such a rite cannot be justified on historical or theological grounds.

Even a nonsacramental understanding of confirmation does not automatically solve all the problems. For instance, in the late 1950s the Lutheran World Federation asked one of its Commissions to study the issue of confirmation. One of the reasons was that questions had emerged whether there must be a rite of confirmation sometime after baptism without which one cannot be admitted to communion, as was customarily assumed in Lutheran circles. Since baptism is incorporation into the body of Christ, there actually should not be a further rite necessary that allows full participation to the body through sharing the eucharistic meal. As we will see later, those baptized as infants should be admitted to the Eucharist as soon as they are able to have a basic understanding of the sacrament.

Yet the charge of laxity leveled against the major denominations by those who do not practice infant baptism must be taken seriously. Lutherans, for instance, do not allow indiscriminate admission to the

Eucharist, but insist on a brief instruction into the meaning of the Eucharist before such admission is granted. Yet even admission to the Eucharist does not do away with the necessity of catechetical instruction.

Perhaps a Roman Catholic position advanced by some that if infant baptism is practiced then confirmation is a necessary supplement is more promising.[49] Confirmation could then be seen as a confession of faith in the midst of the congregation by people who all along have been full members of that community, although now they are able to express this faith on their own and can assume their share of congregational responsibility. This does not mean that baptism is necessarily deficient. It is complete and valid without our own doing. In this way the primacy of God's grace is maintained. Yet at one point or another it will lead to the response from the baptized. Though there is no sacramental rite of confirmation documented in the New Testament, there is also no law which would forbid the ritualization of such response in confirmation.

We have then four moments contained in confirmation: (1) catechetical instruction of those members who were baptized as infants; (2) affirmation of their baptismal faith; (3) assumption of full congregational responsibility (as far as legally permissible); and (4) preparation for first communion. The question, of course, must be raised whether all four moments must always be merged together in one rite or whether some can function independently. Especially the recent Lutheran practice to allow participation in the Eucharist after a brief instruction into the meaning of the Eucharist, usually before confirmation, seems to assume that some points can be separated if theologically or practically mandated. This is even more feasible when confirmation is considered not as a sacrament, but a necessary rite of passage into adult church membership.

THE VALIDITY OF INFANT BAPTISM

Except for the Baptist tradition, most Christian churches today practice infant baptism almost exclusively. Adult baptism occurs then predominantly in missionary settings. One might question whether the practice of infant baptism can be defended on biblical grounds. As we noted, baptism has an active and a passive component; the ones who want to be baptized ask for and then receive baptism. Both the active and the passive moments make up the sacrament. Yet infants are unable to express the desire to be baptized, and they also will not renounce their sinfulness if such can even be ascertained with them. Infant baptism cannot be presupposed as the rule and norm unless we can support it by a sound scriptural basis.

It is common opinion among New Testament scholars today that infant baptism is neither expressly attested or commanded in the New Testament. Nevertheless, Joachim Jeremias in his careful study, *Infant Baptism in the First Four Centuries* (Ger. 1958; Eng. 1960), forcefully advocated infant baptism as a New Testament practice. He detected a parallel between infant baptism of children whose parents converted to Christianity and Jewish proselyte baptism. When parents converted to Judaism, their infants were baptized with them. Several times New Testament writers mention that someone was baptized together with his household (cf. Acts 16:15). While one cannot determine that in every instance infants were involved also, it is safe to assume that in some cases infants must have been included. According to Jeremias the matter may have been different with children of Christian parents, but we do not hear of a separate rite for these children alongside a rite of conversion baptism for adults. It seems that early on Christian-born infants were baptized too. This would coincide with the affinity of the Christian baptism to circumcision (cf. Col. 2:11–12), a rite for infants of Jewish parents.

Similar to Jeremias, Kurt Aland also holds that infant baptism today is not only necessary but legitimate. Yet he sharply disagrees with the approach of Jeremias. In his book, *Did the Early Church Baptize Infants*? (Ger. 1961; Eng. 1963), he dismisses the term "conversion baptism." According to Aland baptism always included a period of preparation through baptismal instruction. As the catechumenate developed more fully one could no longer talk about a direct conversion from paganism to Christianity. The catechumens were already to some extent members. For instance, Emperor Constantine was baptized on his deathbed. Yet his involvement with church matters at the Council of Nicaea and other places indicated that he certainly had been a Christian prior to his baptism. Aland also cites Tertullian who claims that "delay of baptism is preferable; principally, however, in the case of little children."[50] To appreciate Tertullian's position we must understand that baptism implies the forgiveness of all our former sins (Hermas, *Mandates* 4.3.1). Since the notion of a second penance after baptism was not yet clearly developed, baptism was the one and only chance to receive forgiveness of all former sins. The life after baptism was then considered to demand a life of holiness, and it was wisest to be baptized as late as possible.

Though this concept of forgiveness may certainly have been a strong point for cautioning against infant baptism, Aland wants us to consider another point. He refers to Gregory of Nazianzus who still in 381 cautions against early baptism of infants with the words: "I give my advice to wait till the end of the third year, or a little more or less, when they may be able to listen and answer something about the Sacraments: that, even though they do not perfectly understand it, yet at any rate they may know the outlines."[51] Furthermore although Gregory and Tertullian do not reject infant baptism, they do object to baptism of newborn babies. So Aland rightly claims that Jeremias does not really want to address the issue of baptism of young children but of newborn babies.[52] According to Aland such early baptism was not widely practiced until the beginning of the third century. Up until that time one thought that the Parousia would occur at any moment and that Christ would take the sinless babies and infants directly with him into paradise.[53] But once one assumed that the Parousia was not so imminent and that newborn babies were afflicted with original sin, baptism of infants became mandatory. Against this trend, which emerged at the beginning of the third century, Tertullian, and presumably Gregory also, fought in vain.

For Aland, Cyprian typifies the thinking of the church with regard to baptism as it generally emerged in the third century: "The mercy and grace of God is not to be refused to any one born of man. For as the Lord says in his gospel, 'The Son of man is not come to destroy men's lives, but to save them,' as far as we can, we must strive that, if possible, no soul be lost."[54] Aland also sees this to be in harmony with the New Testament. Though the New Testament does not give us mandatory advice when a person must be baptized, it emphasizes that baptism is not founded on our faith but on God's action. Thus God's acceptance of us comes prior to any action on our side. If we baptize on account of someone's faith, uncertainty as to whether this faith was not sincere and deep enough always exists.[55] Sacraments, however, are unwavering signs of God's grace and acceptance. This gives Aland a theological basis to assert the necessity of infant baptism today.

Though both Jeremias and Aland accept infant baptism as valid, Jeremias felt that Aland's assumption of a change in the baptismal practice of the early church warranted a rejoinder. Thus he wrote *The Origins of Infant Baptism. A Further Study in Reply to Kurt Aland* (Ger. 1962; Eng. 1963). Evaluating Aland's arguments Jeremias concludes that one cannot document that in the early church young children were first instructed before they could be baptized. Jeremias agrees with Aland that Tertullian is the first explicit witness to infant baptism, but he emphasizes the context of Tertullian's recommendation that "the delay of baptism is preferable; principally, however, in the case of little children."[56] Tertullian is concerned, here, that the sponsors "may fail to fulfil their promises, and may be disappointed by the development of an evil disposition, *in those for whom they stood*." This argument, that the sponsors might not live up to their promises or that the baptized infants might grow out of the church instead of into it, sounds rather contemporary in the ears of those who today consider infant baptism. Yet for Jeremias what is crucial is that Tertullian mentions that there were sponsors for the infants. This would clearly indicate that in the African church newborn babies were baptized, a practice which Tertullian opposed nevertheless.

Decisive for Jeremias, however, is his theological conclusion.[57] He affirms that in the New Testament the unbaptized infant is sanctified through the baptized parents. This sanctification is not of a moral but an eschatological dimension. Through the parents one comes into relationship with the new creation in Christ. Thus the Christian parents are encouraged to "save" their child, that is, lead him or her to faith and baptism (1 Cor. 7:16). In the New Testament infants are not depicted in innocence without need of God's grace. Furthermore, baptism is not just the washing away of sins. Such a truncated notion led to the delay of baptism in the fourth century. Yet baptism is most prominently an eschatological sacrament. It is not just a rite of new creation, new birth, adoption, being made righteous, etc. In short, baptism involves incorporation into the dominion of Christ, actualized eschatology, and anticipation of the completion of salvation. Such a sacrament does not tolerate a delay. It should be administered as soon as possible to reap its benefits.

While the arguments of Jeremias seem to carry more weight than do Aland's we wonder whether it was just the undue emphasis on baptism as the washing away of sins that led to a delay of baptism. We also must consider that initially in the face of the expected imminent Parousia, the notion of a second penance did not clearly develop. The only chance to obtain forgiveness of all sins was thought to be in baptism. Gradually, however, one realized that the return of Christ was not just around the corner. Then one thought it best to delay baptism as long as possible to reap its benefits—complete forgiveness of sins. When the notion of a second penance emerged, meaning that one could obtain remission of sins even after baptism, there was no need to advocate a delay of baptism. Thus we hear from Cyprian, barely forty years later, almost the opposite argument as that of Tertullian. If God can forgive all sinners who have accumulated the sins of a whole life, how much easier should it be for God to forgive an infant who has no other sin than being born into a sinful context?[58] There should be no discrimination of age, Cyprian argues; God's grace and mercy must not be denied to anyone. Contrary to some contemporary claims, infant baptism as a prevalent practice did not result just from the change from a missionary church to an established one. There were other factors involved, too, such as the general acceptance of a second penance and the growing emphasis on the gravity of original sin. The predominant practice of infant baptism led away from the heavy emphasis on law and sanctification. The church was brought back to a more dynamic and more New Testament–oriented understanding of the continued necessity of grace and forgiveness.

When we consider whether infant baptism is still tenable today we must also assess its forceful renunciation by Karl Barth. In his small booklet, *The Teaching of the Church Regarding Baptism* (1948), he defines Christian baptism as

> the representation (*Abbild*) of a man's renewal through his participation by means of the power of the Holy Spirit in the death and resurrection of Jesus Christ, and therewith the representation of man's association with Christ, with the covenant of grace which is concluded and realised in him, and with the fellowship of His church.[59]

For this representation of renewal, Barth claims, it is not sufficient that an infant is just sprinkled with water or his or her hair moistened; but in analogy to the circumcision of the Old Testament, baptism through immersion should present a real threat to life, followed immediately by the corresponding deliverance and preservation, the raising from baptism. Barth's attack on infant baptism comes from "the Reformed standpoint with its cognitive understanding of baptismal grace."[60] He admits that baptism without willingness and readiness of the baptized is true, effectual, and effective baptism. Unlike Anabaptist usage, he admits that it must not and ought not be repeated, but it is not correct usage. "It is not done in obedience, it is not administered according to proper order, and therefore is necessarily clouded baptism." He claims that today even in the Reformed church the baptismal practice prevalent is "arbitrary and despotic."[61] The person to be baptized is merely a passive instrument, while, according to Barth, it should be "an active partner." "Baptism is in the New Testament in every case the indispensable answer to an unavoidable question by a man who has come to faith. . . . In the sphere of the New Testament one is not brought to baptism; one comes to baptism."[62]

Barth sees in the attempts of Luther and Calvin to justify infant baptism unconvincing arguments that cannot do without exegetical and practical "artifices and sophism."[63] He wonders whether the real reason for infant baptism operative in the Reformers and in the theologians today is the fear that without infant baptism the Constantinian majority church would collapse. Even Luther, he says, once confessed that "there would not be too many people baptized, if, instead of being brought to baptism, they had to come of their own accord."[64] But Barth does not want such practical questions to decide the issue. Since baptism always demands a response on the part of the baptized, he simply wants "instead of the present infant-baptism, a baptism which on the part of the baptized is a responsible act. If it is to be natural, the candidate, instead of being a passive object of baptism, must become once more the free partner of Jesus Christ, that is, freely deciding, freely confessing, declaring on his part his willingness and readiness."[65]

In the last fragmentary volume of his monumental *Church Dogmatics*, Karl Barth again picked up the issue of baptism. In his elaborate discussion he disclaims that baptism is an actual sacrament. Baptism is not God's doing but ours which refers to his doing in Jesus Christ. It is not an instrument of grace, no mystery, and not a sacrament, but we respond in it to the one mystery and sacrament of the history of Jesus Christ—his resurrection and the pouring out of the Holy Spirit. When Barth comes to the issue of infant baptism, his arguments remain basically the same as they were two decades earlier. Infant baptism is the consequence of the Constantinian era in which being a member of the empire gradually became synonymous with being a member of the church. To attain this identification one had to be baptized as early as possible. Such motives are rightly evaluated by Barth as insufficient to warrant infant baptism. Moreover, he recognizes that today the coincidence of empire and church is no longer given.

While we agree with Karl Barth that infant baptism is problematic, we must reject this notion that baptism is not God's doing. On the contrary, it is God's doing and not ours. Yet infant baptism especially can easily become a matter of routine and of tradition providing more the occasion for an elaborate family gathering than for thinking through the consequences of the baptismal covenant. It can also be misunderstood as a magic act by which demons are warded off, or one obtains a life-insurance policy for heaven. Because we are unable to eliminate all possible abuses or misconceptions, we must employ extreme care in practice and theology. First, it must be clear that the church does not baptize all children it can reach, but only children of Christian parents. Furthermore, it does not baptize them in isolation but as sons and daughters of Christian parents and as members of Christian homes. Infant baptism cannot be separated from the context in which the infants and their parents stand. Thus we are not talking here about an isolated child and an isolated baptismal act.

Infant baptism is only to be conducted if the parents or their representatives bring the child to baptism. In analogy to the question posed at an adult baptism: "Do you desire to be baptized?" it is essential in infant baptism to ask both the parents and the sponsors: "Do you desire this child to be baptized and do you promise that he or she will be reared as a member of the Christian community?"[66] After baptism we must not cease to remind the parents of the responsibility that they assumed when they had their infants baptized. It was therefore only proper when Vatican II decreed: "The rite for baptism of infants is to be revised, and should be adapted to the circumstances that those to be baptized are, in fact, infants. The roles of parents and godparents, and also their duties, should be brought out more sharply in the rite itself."[67] Since the parents will ask for baptism, the church may assume that the child will be brought up in the Christian community and encounter God's word. This means that there would exist a situation that makes baptism meaningful and justifiable.

In many places, however, infant baptism has become such a meaningless tradition that responsibility is promised without much thought. Yet similar problems are encountered in traditions that insist on adult baptism. As Paul indicated with his imperatives following the indicative of a new existence through baptism, it is always necessary for the church to remind the parents of their obligation and to see to it that the children are indeed instructed in the Christian faith. If we would opt for adult baptism as the rule, we would not actually revert to ancient Christian practice as most advocates of adult baptism surmise.[68] Moreover, the unbaptized infants or adolescents would not grow up in a non-Christian religion and then, through confrontation with the Christian gospel, make a conscientious decision for the Christian faith. In all likelihood they would grow up in a secular culture and indifferent to metaphysical values. Thus a renunciation of other gods and a pledge of allegiance to the Christian God would be highly improbable.

When Karl Barth asks for baptism in which the candidate is "an active partner . . . freely deciding, freely confessing," one may wonder whether the emphasis is still on the primacy of God's grace and his action. As soon as the main attention focuses on our doing, uncertainty creeps in because we do not know whether we did enough or whether we made a profound enough confession. Yet Barth touched on a significant point. Our response to the grace offered in baptism is important. Without it baptism is incomplete, unless we would grant a mechanistic view of infusion of grace through infant baptism. It is interesting that the Heidelberg Catechism explicitly deals with the issue, "are infants also to be baptized?" and affirms it without reservations, with the remark that "infants are also by baptism, as a sign of the covenant, to be incorporated into the Christian church and distinguished from the children of unbelievers."[69] Yet presumably under the influence of Barth, the contemporary commentary comes to the conclusion that "the danger of making people indifferent" to a confessional stand is greater with infant baptism that with adult baptism.[70]

When in early Christianity so many adults flocked to the church, infants may indeed have not received the attention in baptism that they deserved. But today with subsequent baptismal instruction for children the situation is different. Today the proper place for adult baptism is the mission field where baptism actually implies a conversion. In other places adult baptism implies no more and no less a confessional situation as does infant baptism. This becomes especially clear in some socialist countries in which infant baptism and subsequent confirmation deprive the children of many educational and professional opportunities while postponement of baptism until adulthood helps them escape such confessional consequences. In such situations adult baptism is an understandable decision to circumvent the desired oppression of believers by an officially atheistic government.

To alleviate the fear of a mechanistic understanding, the Reformers devised all kinds of theories to justify infant baptism, as we see in Luther's case.[71] Yet none of these sufficed. At the end, it was very clear for Luther that baptism is totally God's gift. It summons us to faith and its reality and validity do not depend on our own disposition.

In baptism God acts with us by incorporating us into the salvational benefits of Christ.[72] We do nothing in baptism; God does everything. Infant baptism is grounded in the sole activity of God in Christ Jesus. Yet this passive aspect on our side always necessitates and incites our active response. When Martin Luther therefore asked in his Small Catechism, "What does such baptizing with water signify?" he responded, "It signifies that the old Adam in us, together with all sins and evil lusts, should be drowned by daily sorrow and repentance and be put to death, and that the new man should come forth daily and rise up, cleansed and righteous, to live forever in God's presence."[73] Baptism, though singular and efficacious without our own doing, is a never-finished process. It will continuously be appropriated. Similar to sanctification growing out of the experience of justification, the appropriation of the baptismal grace grows out of baptism. Yet such appropriation is not to be construed as a precondition for the sacrament's efficacy. If it were so, we could never be certain of its efficacy. It is rather a response to God's action.

In conclusion to our reflections on baptism it would be helpful to listen to some of the statements of the Faith and Order Commission of the World Council of Churches in the so-called Lima text. This document was sent to participating churches for reflection and comments and picks up very well our own concerns. It states:

> Baptism is the sign of new life through Jesus Christ. . . . Administered in obedience to our Lord, baptism is a sign and seal of our common discipleship. Through baptism, Christians are brought into union with Christ, with each other and with the Church of every time and place. . . . Baptism is an unrepeatable act. Any practice which might be interpreted as "re-baptism" must be avoided. . . . Believer baptists and those who practise infant baptism should reconsider certain aspects of their practices. The first may seek to express more visibly the fact that children are placed under the protection of God's grace. The latter must guard themselves against the practice of apparently indiscriminate baptism and take more seriously their responsibility for the nurture of baptized children to mature commitment to Christ.[74]

Since baptism is God's gift it is not to be administered lightly. This is also true in the case of emergency baptism when an infant who has not been baptized is in a life-threatening situation. Barth is certainly right when he declares that "the power of Jesus Christ . . . is not dependent upon the carrying out of baptism."[75] Therefore we should not categorically insist on emergency baptism. Since baptism means also incorporation into the visible and invisible body of Christ, the incorporation into the visible church would be of such short duration that it would lose its meaning. If we look for any response to the baptismal grace, we can also not expect it in this life if the infant dies soon thereafter. Thus emergency baptism would carry solely passive aspects unless we reflect on the desires of the parents or sponsors. But baptism is also the incorporation into the church as the New Covenant community, something which extends beyond death. It is not just a rite that pertains to this life only. Emergency baptism should not be denied if it is sincerely desired. But it is much more a pastoral act for the sake of the good conscience of the next of kin, that nothing was left undone to assure the infant's salvation, than a theologically necessary one, for the sake of the infant's salvation.

NOTES

1. Heidelberg Catechism (question 68), 117.
2. Martin Luther, Large Catechism, in *BC*, 436.
3. Philip Melanchthon, Apology of the Augsburg Confession (XIII), in *BC*, 211, where he quotes his *Loci* of 1521.
4. Raphael Schulte, "Sacraments," in *Sacramentum Mundi* 5:378.
5. Karl Rahner, "The Word and the Eucharist," in *Theological Investigations*, vol. 4: *More Recent Writings*, trans. K. Smyth (New York: Helicon Press, 1966), 274.
6. Tertullian *To the Martyrs* (3.1), in FC 40:22.
7. Justin Martyr *The First Apology* (66), in ANF 1:185.
8. Tertullian *On Prescription against Heretics* (40), in ANF 3:262.
9. John Chrysostom *Homily 15 (John 1.18)*, in FC 33:150.
10. "Decree for the Armenians" (695), in Heinrich Denzinger, *The Sources of Catholic Dogma*, trans. R. J. Deferrari (St. Louis: B. Herder, 1957), 220.
11. Ibid., 221.
12. According to Jaroslav Pelikan, *The Christian Tradition. A History of*

the Development of Doctrine, vol. 3: *The Growth of Medieval Theology (600–1300)* (Chicago and London: University of Chicago Press, 1978), 207.

13. Augustine *Reply to Faustus the Manichaean* (19.16), in NPNF 4:245.

14. For this and the following quote, see Augustine *On the Gospel of St. John* (80.3), in NPNF 7:344, in his exegesis of John 15:1–3.

15. Martin Luther, Small Catechism (4.3), in *BC*, 349.

16. "Canons of the Sacraments in General" (849), in Denzinger, *Sources of Catholic Dogma*, 262.

17. Ibid. (851), 263.

18. Karl Rahner, "The Word and the Eucharist," 274.

19. Raphael Schulte, "Sacraments (in general)," in *Sacramentum Mundi* 5:380.

20. Luther, Small Catechism (4.3), in *BC*, 349.

21. Schulte, "Sacraments (in general)," 380.

22. Lutheran/Roman Catholic Joint Commission, *The Eucharist* (Geneva: Lutheran World Federation, 1980), 22.

23. For this and the following quote, see "Foreword to the Sacraments" (843a and 847), in Denzinger, *Sources of Catholic Dogma*, 262.

24. Philip Melanchthon, Apology of the Augsburg Confession (13), in *BC*, 212.

25. Gottfried Thomasius, *Christi Person und Werk*, vol. 3/2: *Das Werk des Mittlers* (Erlangen: Theodor Bläsing, 1861), 117.

26. Cf. Ernst Haenchen, *Die Apostelgeschichte*, 11th ed. (Göttingen: Vandenhoeck & Ruprecht, 1959), 254, who in his exegesis of Acts 8:17, mentions that in the Lukan congregations baptism and laying on of hands seem to be connected. Only later the laying on of hands was separated from baptism and continued as the rite of confirmation. Yet Tertullian still mentions the laying on of hands in connection with baptism. To make out of the laying on of hands already in the New Testament a separate rite of "the post-baptismal gift of the Spirit" as advocated by J. Ysebaert, *Greek Baptismal Terminology. Its Origin and its Early Development* (Nijmwegen: Dekker & Van de Vegt, 1962), 262, is unwarranted.

27. Cf. Otto Michel, *Der Brief an die Römer*, 10th ed. (Göttingen: Vandenhoeck & Ruprecht, 1957), 139–40, in his excursus on the peculiarity of Paul's understanding of baptism. That Romans 6 has nothing whatsoever to do with a mystery scheme, as suggested by Günter Wagner, *Pauline Baptism and the Pagan Mysteries. The Problem of the Pauline Doctrine of Baptism in Romans VI. 1–11, in the Light of its Religio-Historical "Parallels"*, trans. J. P. Smith (Edinburgh: Oliver & Boyd, 1967), seems to be overstating the

case. Yet his observation has to be taken seriously that he has not been able "to trace a single text or allusion from the Apostolic and Church Fathers in which Rom VI was interpreted by reference to or in contrast with 'analogous' rites or experiences of the *mystai* of Attis, Adonis, or Osiris," (ibid., 285). Obviously Christian theologians did not perceive the mysteries as a threat to baptism as they did to the Eucharist. One of the reasons may have been the clear understanding that baptism was not just a symbol, however realistically it might have been viewed. It marked the break in the life of the person baptized which took place in the passing from the non-Christian to the Christian state. The baptized one indeed became a new being.

28. For the following, cf. the instructive essay by Erich Dinkler, "Die Taufterminologie in 2 Kor 1,21f.," in *Signum Crucis* (Tübingen: J. C. B. Mohr [Paul Siebeck], 1967), 99–117.

29. For the discussion of this passage, cf. Hans Conzelmann, *1 Corinthians*, trans. James W. Leitch (Philadelphia: Fortress Press, 1975), 121ff., who refers also to the differing view of Joachim Jeremias.

30. So Georg Kretschmar, *Studien zur frühchristlichen Trinitätstheologie* (Tübingen: J. C. B. Mohr [Paul Siebeck], 1956), 206–7. Once the relationship between Father, Son, and Holy Spirit had received sufficient clarification, it was only natural that one was baptized in the name of all three, indicating their oneness, instead of the name of Jesus alone. Through baptism one then became the property of the Trinity and therewith of Christ.

31. R. A. Barclay, "New Testament Baptism. An External or Internal Rite?" in *Initiation*, ed. C. J. Bleeker (Leiden: E. J. Brill, 1965), 183.

32. Luther, Large Catechism (Baptism), in *BC*, 446.

33. For this and the following quote, see Luther, Small Catechism (4.4), in *BC*, 349.

34. Barclay, "New Testament Baptism," 183. For the significance of baptism today, cf. the excellent book by George Beasley-Murray, *Baptism Today and Tomorrow* (New York: St. Martin's Press, 1966), which is written from an informed and ecumenically minded Baptist perspective.

35. Luther, Small Catechism (Apostles' Creed), in *BC*, 345.

36. Basil the Great *On the Spirit* (12:28), in NPNF, second series 8:18.

37. Michael Schmaus, *Der Glaube der Kirche, Handbuch katholischer Dogmatik* (Munich: Max Hueber, 1970), 2:423.

38. For a good survey of the history of confirmation, see Wilhelm Maurer, "Geschichte von Firmung und Konfirmation bis zum Ausgang der lutherischen Orthodoxie," in *Confirmatio. Forschungen zur Geschichte und Praxis der Konfirmation*, ed. Kurt Frör (Munich: Evang. Presseverband, 1959), 9–38. For the Roman Catholic position, cf. the excellent book by

Jean Amougou-Atangana, *Ein Sakrament des Geistempfangs? Zum Verhältnis von Taufe und Firmung* (Freiburg: Herder, 1974). For a popular account in English, see the study book *Confirmation and First Communion*, ed. Frank W. Klos (Minneapolis: Augsburg, 1968).

39. Denzinger, *Sources of Catholic Dogma*, 222.

40. "Canon on the Sacrament of Confirmation" (871 and 873), in ibid., 265.

41. "Constitution on the Sacred Liturgy" (71), in *The Documents of Vatican II*, ed. Walter M. Abbott (New York: Association Press, 1966), 160.

42. "Decree on Eastern Catholic Churches" (12f.), in ibid., 379.

43. As translated in the excellent collection by J. D. C. Fisher, *Christian Initiation. Some Early Reformed Rites of Baptism and Confirmation and Other Contemporary Documents* (London: SPCK, 1970), 173.

44. As translated in ibid., 254.

45. As translated in ibid., 258 (*Institutes*, ed. 1536, IV.19.13).

46. So Fisher, ibid., 260.

47. For details and the text of these orders, see ibid., 174–81.

48. Piet Fransen, "Confirmation," in *Sacramentum Mundi* 1:409.

49. The conclusion in Jean Amougou-Atangana's investigation shows an amazing ecumenical openness. Yet we wonder whether one can talk about confirmation as "a supplement to a [in itself deficient] infant baptism" (*Ein Sakrament des Geistempfangs?* 312). Baptism even as infant baptism is not deficient. But the catechumenate, which in connection with baptism was so important in the early church, cannot be omitted. In this way confirmation signifies the conclusion of this catechumenate.

50. Tertullian *On Baptism* (18), in ANF 3:678.

51. Gregory of Nazianzus *Oration on Holy Baptism* (28), in NPNF, second series 7:370.

52. Kurt Aland, *Did the Early Church Baptize Infants?* trans. G. R. Beasley-Murray (Philadelphia: Westminster Press, 1963) 30–31.

53. Ibid., 106.

54. Cyprian *Epistles* (58.2), in ANF 5:354.

55. Cf. Aland, *Did the Early Church Baptize Infants?* 112–13, especially the quotations from Luther which highlight Aland's and our misgivings about a baptism preceded by a confession of one's faith.

56. Joachim Jeremias, *The Origins of Infant Baptism: A Further Study in Reply to Kurt Aland*, trans. Dorothea M. Barton (Naperville, Ill.: Alec R. Allenson, 1963), 64–65.

57. For this paragraph and the next, cf. ibid., 76–77.

58. Cf. Cyprian *Epistles* (64.5), in FC 51:218–19.

59. Karl Barth, *The Teaching of the Church Regarding Baptism*, trans. E. A. Payne (London: SCM Press, 1948), 9.

60. For this and the following quote, see ibid., 40.

61. For this and the following quote, see ibid., 41.

62. Ibid., 42.

63. Ibid., 49.

64. Ibid., 53.

65. Ibid., 54.

66. This is made specific when the minister addresses parents and sponsors of young children in the Order of Holy Baptism in the *LBW*: "You should, therefore, faithfully bring them to the services of God's house, and teach them the Lord's Prayer, the Creed, and the Ten Commandments. As they grow in years, you should place in their hands the Holy Scriptures and provide for their instruction in the Christian faith, that living in the covenant of their Baptism and in communion with the Church, they may lead godly lives until the day of Jesus Christ. Do you promise to fulfill these obligations?" (121).

67. "Constitution on the Sacred Liturgy" (67), *The Documents of Vatican II*, 160.

68. George R. Beasley-Murray, *Baptism in the New Testament* (New York: Macmillan Co., 1962), presents a very learned and careful approach to the issue of infant baptism. Yet he wrongly assumes that with his advocacy of adult "conversion" baptism he is on New Testament ground.

69. The Heidelberg Catechism (question 74), 122.

70. Ibid., 127.

71. For details, cf. Paul Althaus, *The Theology of Martin Luther*, trans. R. C. Schultz (Philadelphia: Fortress Press, 1966), 364–70.

72. For the following, cf. the thoughtful comments by Gerhard Delling, "Zur Taufe von 'Häusern' im Urchristentum," in *Studien zum Neuen Testament und zum hellenistischen Judentum. Gesammelte Aufsätze 1950–1968* (Göttingen: Vandenhoeck & Ruprecht, 1970), 310.

73. Luther, Small Catechism (The Sacrament of Holy Baptism), in *BC*, 349.

74. *Baptism, Eucharist and Ministry*, Faith and Order Paper No. 111 (Geneva: World Council of Churches, 1982), 2–6 (2, 6, 13, 16).

75. Barth, *The Teaching of the Church Regarding Baptism*, 23.

4

The Lord's Supper

As with baptism, the Lord's Supper was also instituted as a Christian sacrament through the experience of the resurrected Christ, although its origin dates back to the experience of Jesus of Nazareth. The development of the Eucharist had to fight two main temptations: to arrive at an ever-greater specificity in describing the Lord's presence and to turn the sacrament into an instrument of the church through which saving grace could be secured. During the Reformation the major issue was the proper distinction between and interpretation of outward sign and inward effect. Jesus gives himself truly to each of the participants in his love sacrifice and therewith gathers and strengthens the Christian community as his living body assuring them in the hope of eternal life. Ordination to ministry regulates and facilitates the administration of word and sacraments.

THE BIBLICAL FOUNDATION OF THE LORD'S SUPPER

Along with the ministerial office and the apostolic succession, the Lord's Supper is one of the main points of disagreement among different denominations.[1] As with other breakthroughs in ecumenical discussions, progress in a basic agreement of the Lord's Supper can only be reached if we ask again for the biblical basis of our understanding of the Lord's Supper, or, even more pointedly, if we ask for the common root(s) out of which these differing interpretations grew. While historical and liturgical considerations should not be omitted, all denominations seem to find a basis for their differences in the New Testament. This fact contains both a promise, since it directs us to the New Testament as a common source, and a problem, since it symptomatically shows that consensus upon the New Testament accounts of the Lord's Supper has not yet been attained. Nevertheless, there are some basic agreements that we should not overlook.

Most would agree that we have four accounts of the institution of the Lord's Supper, all of which show liturgical use:

1. The oldest document in which the words of the institution of the Lord's Supper are recorded is Paul's First Letter to the Corinthians, most likely dating back to the spring of A.D. 54 (1 Cor. 11:23–25). When Paul writes: "I received from the Lord what I also delivered to you," we notice that he has previously told the congregation about the Lord's Supper and is now making reference to it. The mentioning of "I received" and "I delivered" reminds them that this was not his own rendering, but, in analogy to rabbinic custom, an authoritative teaching tradition. As Paul has indicated with the phrase "from the Lord," its origin must be sought in a time much earlier than A.D. 54, going back beyond the Christian community to the Lord himself.

2. The second oldest literary source is Mark 14:22–25, which
3. we find again with minor modifications in Matt. 26:26–29.

4. A tradition which has aroused much debate is that preserved in Luke 22:15–20. This version is analogous to the versions found in Mark, Matthew, and Paul. A shorter version of the same text also exists, which stops abruptly after the words: "and he took bread, and when he had given thanks he broke it and gave it to them, saying, 'This is my body'" (Luke 22:19). Usually a shorter text is considered to be the older one, but here it is impossible to assume that with the shorter version Luke would advocate the communion with bread only, since two verses earlier he explicitly stated communion with wine when he mentioned that Jesus, "took a cup, and when he had given thanks he said, 'Take this, and divide it among yourselves'" (Luke 22:17). Since more of the older manuscripts witness to its existence as well, the longer text must be considered the older one.[2] The shorter text may owe its existence to the arcanum discipline. That is, the attempt was made to recite only the beginning words of

the institution of the Lord's Supper, thereby leaving the uninitiated in the dark concerning its exact meaning.

The Gospel of John does not mention the words of institution explicitly, perhaps again for fear that its text might come into the hands of the wrong people. Yet it refers to the eating and drinking of Jesus' flesh and blood, and it contains the promise that those who do this will have eternal life and that God will raise them up at the last day (John 6:51b–58).

The fact that the Lord's Supper is documented in the major New Testament sources shows its significance. Yet how far back can we trace its tradition? Matthew seems to present only a variation of Mark, and Luke seems to be more original than Paul. The many Semitisms in Mark indicate that it is older than Luke. But Mark itself is an emendation of an earlier version. It may be safe to assume that while we do not have access to the oldest version, there are two (Paul and Mark) or even three (Paul, Mark, and John) distinct traditions, all going back to the original Hebrew or Aramaic version and agreeing in their basic content. This would imply that the New Testament has preserved a tradition that in all likelihood goes back to Jesus himself.

When we consider the accounts of the institution we notice that they developed from a common root into different liturgical traditions. In all likelihood we can ascertain that this root contained at least five parts:[3]

1. An introduction along with the reference to the praise over the bread at the beginning and the prayer of thanks over the cup at the end of the meal.

2. The word over the distributed bread: "This is my body."

3. The reference to the meal which had taken place.

4. The word about the cup in the Pauline-Lukan form: "This cup (which is poured out for you) is the new covenant in my blood."

5. The eschatological outlook which is preserved in its main part in Mark 14:25 ("Truly, I say to you, I shall not drink again of the fruit of the vine until that day I drink it new in the kingdom of God").

The elaborations in the different accounts can then be understood as consequent interpretations of this common root. Yet before we elaborate on the significance of the Lord's Supper we must consider Jesus' last supper and the lasting theological relevance its date might have.

According to the Synoptics the last supper was a Passover meal. John, however, tells us that Jesus died the same afternoon the Passover lambs were slaughtered, meaning that the general Passover meal took place the evening after Jesus' death. One could argue, however, that there were different calendars concerning the Passover. Therefore John could be right when he implies that Jesus died on Friday, the day of the general Passover, while the Synoptics were also right in recording that Jesus celebrated his last supper as Passover meal (i.e., a day earlier than those who had their lambs slaughtered at the temple).[4] Yet the theological significance is not primarily dependent on establishing the exact date of the last supper.[5] Even if the last supper took place as a Passover meal, which is most likely, Jesus could have given the meal a totally new content from what was to be expected.

The most important difference between the Passover meal and the Lord's Supper was that the former was celebrated only once a year, while the latter was celebrated daily, or at least weekly. In this difference in use (remembering the exodus from Egypt versus remembering the death of Jesus) we see a very different theological understanding of the last supper.

The question of a dependence on the Passover tradition within Judaism is irrelevant insofar as this tradition does not form a constitutive element of the Lord's Supper of the first Christian community.[6] Nevertheless there were certainly some connections drawn between the Passover and the Lord's Supper. In Jewish Christian circles the custom of celebrating annually a Christianized Passover in connection with a celebration of the Lord's Supper continued well into the second century, as seen in the Quartodeciman practice. This group of Christians in Asia Minor and Syria celebrated the Passover parallel to the Jews on the evening of the fourteenth of Nisan and the night of the fifteenth. They fasted for the Jews, read and explained the Passover narrative in Exodus, and expected the return of the Messiah.[7] At the first cock crow the fasting ended, and the agape meal and the Eucharist in which the Lord was united with his followers commenced. Among Hellenistic Christians, however, the notion became prevalent that the resurrection of the Lord and the Eucharist should be celebrated on the first Sunday after the fourteenth of Nisan, thereby making a bigger distinction between the Christian Eucharist and the Jewish Passover by celebrating them on different days and also giving more emphasis to the original day of the week of the resurrection.

While the Quartodecimans may have preserved the memory of the original last supper, the Hellenistic church whose view eventually prevailed was right when it demanded a clear distinction between the church of the resurrection and the Judaism of waiting and hope. The question must be asked, however, whether today such explicit demarcation over against Judaism is still necessary or whether the common roots of our hope, intimately grounded in the exodus event, should not gain more emphasis. This question is especially important since in many Christian circles the idea of a Seder or Passover meal is gaining new popularity. In showing the preliminary character of the exodus event, such a meal can enhance our understanding of Jewish analogies to the Eucharist without compromising the Christian gospel. As a Passover meal, it is not a Christian rite and therefore it is mainly of historical interest for us.

When we come to the theological significance of the Lord's Supper then, to obtain a full understanding, we must consider alongside Jesus' last supper the meals that he also shared daily with his disciples and the meals he had with sinners and outcasts of society. It was important for the first Christian community that the Lord's Supper was connected with an actual meal. As Jesus shared with them, they shared with each other and, albeit in a different way, with those outside their community. Yet soon we notice a shift. The meal no longer took place between the breaking of the bread and the drinking of the cup but often prior to both. Nevertheless, up until the middle of the second century the connection between a meal and the Lord's Supper is commonly accepted. As a third component one must also consider the strong faith in the resurrected and exalted One, the expectation of his Parousia and of the completion of salvation. These moments were decisive for the understanding of the eucharistic community and the significance of bread and wine. Only the joining of these three components, the last supper, the meals of Jesus, and the experience of the resurrected One, constitutes the celebration of the Lord's supper in the first Christian community.[8]

The Lord's Supper thus includes present, past, and future. It is proclamation of the substitutionary death of Jesus which occurred once and for all for the forgiveness of sins and the establishing of a new order of salvation (the New Covenant). It is celebration of the community of the faithful with their Lord and with one another. It is anticipation of the completed rule of God and it is celebrated with eschatological praise and expectation. This means there are three aspects: christological, ecclesiological, and eschatological. All three must be balanced with each other. Yet this balance was exactly the problem when the church with its Jewish and Hellenistic thought forms wanted to express the significance of the Lord's Supper for its own day.

MAJOR STEPS IN THE DEVELOPMENT OF THE EUCHARIST

The New Testament understanding of the Eucharist is derived from common roots. But it is not uniform in interpreting this tradition. When the Synoptic writers present the last supper of Jesus, they know that Jesus of Nazareth, who was going to die, had become the living, present Christ from whose hands we receive participation in the new salvational order. In all its diversity, Paul and John agree with this account when they tell us that the resurrected and ascended Christ gives himself to his people in his humanity which he sacrificed for them. They receive him, and thus they receive new life. Jesus himself is the means of immortality in his person and in his word. Yet the church's understanding of the Eucharist did not stay within that New Testament conceptuality. Once it ventured into the Hellenistic world, ultimately conquering it, the church also adopted and adapted the conceptual tools of the new environment.

The early church did not develop a dogma of the Lord's Supper in the strict sense of the word.[9] There were no large-scale discussions about it and there were no synodical decrees on it. No special theological treatises on it exist, but only numerous and relatively scattered references. Yet the Lord's Supper stands at the center of the early church's faith and life. In a single rite it embodies and proclaims the entire gospel.

Since many of the newly converted had prior affinities to the Jewish faith, the Lord's Supper was seen in analogy to Jewish meals of fellowship with the blessings said at table. Also the analogy between the commemoration of the redemption from Egypt and the commemoration of redemption on the cross gained new attention. For Christians the Lord's Supper was a focus of their fellowship, the ground and expression of the church's unity in Christ, and of the love that binds the church together. Though the agape meals (love feasts) were gradually celebrated separately, the idea of agape was still prominent. The Lord's Supper was also the Christians' corporate act of thanksgiving for the saving events of Christ's death and resurrection by which the people had been reconciled to God, and God's creation had been rescued from the dominion of evil and assured of the hope of restoration. Since thanksgiving and sacrifice were closely related, the Lord's Supper became the church's offering of praise, blessing, and self-dedication, and an expression of practical service to others. "The offerings of the gifts" were the source and symbol of the church's provision for its poor and needy. Thanksgiving then was not just a commemoration of God's past acts. It centered upon the present communion with the crucified and risen Lord.

It is crucial to remember this summary of communion practice when we now sample a few of the explicit statements by theologians of the early church. If we read their assertions with our own conceptuality in mind, they can easily become the "ammunition dump for later eucharistic controversies."[10] Particularly in the controversies of the sixteenth and seventeenth centuries, theologians of all the major denominations sought support for their point of view in the statements of the patristic age. Yet the exclusive opposition between realism and symbolism, though important in these controversies, was not yet felt in the early church. A symbol was largely understood as an image containing the reality of that which was depicted. As background, for instance, we must bear in mind Philo's spiritual interpretation of the Old Testament sacrifices. And in terms of context we must also remember the Marcionite and Gnostic rejection of the created world in favor of the spiritual realm. Furthermore, we must distinguish between the time before the Christian faith became the established religion, when membership in the Christian community meant participation in the Eucharist, and the time after the Christian faith became the established religion, when worship services assumed an almost public dimension and often the number of communing members was considerably smaller than of those who participated in public worship. Since the number of people receiving instruction in the Christian faith far exceeded those who were admitted to Communion, a different understanding of the Lord's Supper was deemed necessary.

Pre-Nicene Developments

The term "Eucharist," meaning the Lord's Supper as the Christian worship service first in the Greek church (*eucharistia*) and later in the Latin church (*sacramentum eucharistiae*), is a translation of the Hebrew *berakah* ("blessing, gift, thanksgiving"). Initially it denoted the table prayer spoken in praise of God. But soon there developed a specifically Christian use, denoting by the term "Eucharist" the elements of bread and wine over which God had been praised. For instance, Ignatius calls the Eucharist a "gift of God" and defines it "to be the flesh of our Saviour Jesus Christ" (*Smyr.* 7:1).

The early church tried to understand the salvational act of God in Christ and the new reality of the church by "finding" it in the sacred Scripture. In this way it attempted to legitimate them against the Jews as well as against the pagans. Since the words of institution are connected in the Gospels with the Passover it was fitting to perceive the Eucharist in analogy to the rescue of the people of God by night from Egypt. In typological fashion Jesus thus becomes the rock who gives spiritual water, he is the bread from heaven, the true Passover, and the actual high priest. Showing the superiority of Jesus Christ and his sacrifice, Cyprian asks rhetorically: "For who is more a priest of the most high God than our Lord Jesus Christ, who offered a sacrifice to God the Father, and offered that very same thing which Melchizedek had offered, that is, bread and wine, to wit, his body and blood?"[11]

A decisive text, especially in replacing Jewish worship with Christian, was the prophecy in Mal. 1:11: "For from the rising of the sun to its setting my name is great among the nations, and in every place incense is offered to my name, and a pure offering; for my name is great among the nations, says the Lord of hosts." For instance, Justin Martyr tells the Jew Trypho that this passage speaks "of those Gentiles, namely us, who in every place offer sacrifices to him, i.e., the bread of the Eucharist, and also the cup, affirming both that we glorify his name, and that you profane it."[12] This reference also occurs in many other later writers.[13] As we hear in the same passage the Eucharist has cosmic significance, for at the same time we "thank God for having created the world, with all things therein, for the sake of man, and for delivering us from the evil in which we were, and for utterly overthrowing principalities and powers by Him who suffered according to his will." This thanksgiving for creation supplies Justin with a powerful weapon against Gnostic and Marcionite dualism. The offering of bread and wine does not mean that God is in need of anything. Rather, it is offered in thanksgiving for the creation and as a sanctification of created things. We offer to God what is actually his own and thereby proclaim the union of flesh with the Spirit.

The frequently used analogy between Christ's presence in the Eucharist and the incarnation follows a similar direction. Justin Martyr says: "But in like manner as Jesus Christ our Saviour, having been made flesh by the Word of God, had both flesh and blood for our salvation, so likewise have we been taught that the food which is blessed by the prayer of his word and from which our blood and flesh by transmutation are nourished, is the flesh and blood of that Jesus who was made flesh."[14] In analogy to the Logos creating for himself a body to disclose himself to humanity in space and time, so Jesus Christ promised his existence in space and time through his word in connection with bread and wine in order to give us his transforming salvation. Irenaeus argues along similar lines when he states, over against the Valentinian Gnostics and the Ebionites, that God does not despise the creation and he will also redeem it. "He has acknowledged the cup (which is part of the creation) as his own blood, from which he bedews our blood; and the bread (also a part of creation) he has established as his own body, from which he gives increase to our bodies."[15] Even such crassly realistic pronouncements that the breaking of the bread is "the medicine of immortality, the antidote that we would not die, but live forever in Jesus Christ" (Ignatius, *Eph.* 20:2) do not mean that some kind of magic is introduced here by which we obtain immortality. They rather seek to tell us that the bodily dimension of our life is not depised by God. By receiving Christ we, and this also means our bodies, receive his Spirit, eternal life, and the hope in the future resurrection. That this has often been understood differently, especially in popular piety, is quite a different matter.

But even the Christians did not understand so easily that matter and Spirit should not be separated.[16] This we notice in the so-called blessing. In the Jewish *berakah* God is praised as the Creator. The Christians soon took over this custom to develop it into a blessing over the elements in the Eucharist. This implied that the presence of Christ in the Eucharist, and more specifically in bread and wine, was no longer understood as a natural and created order. It had to be prayed for.

This leads to the question of the mode by which the elements are thus identified with what they signify. The life-giving bread which came down from heaven and which was typified by the manna, or the blood of his reconciling sacrifice which was prefigured by the water from the rock, shows that our kind of realism or literalism was yet unknown. By infusion of divine power the elements become "holy" and channels of divine energy. They become "medicine of immortality." When we read in Tertullian that "the flesh feeds on the body and blood of Christ, that the soul likewise may fatten on its God,"[17] we notice a parallelism between a bodily action and a spiritual one. When we read in Ignatius that he desires "the bread of God, the heavenly bread, the bread of life, which is the flesh of Jesus Christ" and the "drink of God, namely his blood, which is incorruptible love and eternal life" (*Rom.* 7:3), we again see that the alternative materialism/spiritualism does not suffice. Irenaeus perhaps expressed this best when he stated: "For as the bread, which is produced from the earth, when it receives the invocation of God, is no longer common bread, but the Eucharist, consisting of two realities, earthly and heavenly; so also our bodies, when they receive the Eucharist, are no longer corruptible, having the hope of the resurrection to eternity."[18] Through his insistence on the material objects of the elements his anti-Marcionite and anti-Gnostic polemic is obvious. But equally obvious is the dual character which guards against mechanistic use. The word has become flesh and is true food, while the material food will only nourish the body. The word said over it will benefit the worthy eater and he will live forever.

Post-Nicene Developments

But how does one worthily receive the Eucharist? This in particular was the question once the church had gained majority status. Now the ecclesial community no longer coincided with the eucharistic community. Since the church was no longer a separate social community, the question of what it meant to be a Christian in a largely "Christian" state emerged. Here the eucharistic community provided the means through which the individual Christian could express his increasing dedication to Christ who offered himself to the faithful in the Eucharist. Since Christ was increasingly thought to be present in a personal way, it was only consequent that one approached the eucharistic table "with fear and trembling." Thus participation in the Eucharist was thought to be more of a privilege for an individual Christian than a matter of fact. Moreover, the Eucharist was depicted more and more as the mystery of the holy, something which is not accessible to rational inquiry.

While the great theologians of the fourth and fifth centuries have in common the fact that they rediscovered Paul in their reflections on the Eucharist, there are two distinct lines of development noticeable: an Eastern one, initiated by the great Cappadocians and completed by John of Damascus, and a Western one, decisively advanced by Ambrose and his famous student Augustine.

The Eastern Emphasis on Deification. Reading in Gregory of Nyssa's *Great Catechism* we first notice the familiar analogy between incarnation and the Eucharist. Gregory declares that Jesus' "body also by the indwelling of God the Word was transmuted to the dignity of Godhead. Rightly, then, do we believe that now also the bread which is consecrated by the Word of God is changed into the Body of God the Word."[19] Also important is the consecration that effects the change in the elements. Of course, this does not mean a change as it was defined later through the term "transubstantiation." It is rather an indwelling similar to God's dwelling in the man Jesus. Yet further in the same chapter we read:

> Since, then, that God-containing flesh partook for its substance and support of this particular nourishment also, and since the God who was manifested infused himself into perishable humanity for this purpose, *viz.* that by this communion with Deity mankind might at the same time be deified, for this end it is that, by dispensation of his grace, he disseminates himself in every believer through that flesh, whose substance comes from bread and wine, blending himself with the bodies of believers, to secure that, by this union with the immortal, man, too, may be a sharer in incorruption.

Of course, we could still understand this in terms of Ingatius's assertion that Christ will dwell in us so that our body will be preserved for new life in the hereafter. Gregory certainly meant that too. But much more important for him is an actual transformation of the faithful through participation in the *logos*. This kind of deification became a major theme in Easter piety.

Parenthetically one should at least mention the influence of language. The Greek language, not to mention the Greek mind, was much more oriented toward being (ontology) than the Latin West with its preoccupation with more legal and analytical categories. The consequences of this kind of thinking in the East were clear. If any reality at all should pertain to the Eucharist it must also express itself in ontological categories.

Another point that was developed with vigor in the East was the analogy between the symbol and that which is symbolized, or between image and reality. John of Damascus particularly elaborates on the relationship between image and that which is imaged. We are created in God's image and as his images we must show reverence to each other since, as John tells us with a quote from Basil the Great, "the honour given to the image passes over to the prototype."[20] A prototype is that which is imaged, from which the derivative is obtained. Consequently, when we worship the cross of Christ, the nails, the spear, the clothes, the manger, and the tomb, we do not worship graven images as the pagans do, but honour them as a symbol of Christ "for wherever the sign may be, there also will He be."[21] All these various signs or means of grace essentially point to Christ, the incarnate representation of God. The idea that the symbol represents that for which it stands and that one obtains with it access to the thing itself led to a multitude of ways in which one could assure divine presence and help. The most important for us here is the use of the sacraments.

In baptism the gift (remission of sins) and the task (regeneration and sanctification) are equally present. Since the Spirit is the active agent in baptism, we are not confronted with a simple moralism. Life after baptism is understood as a dynamic progression toward holiness. Though there is remission of sins even after baptism, we should remember that in baptism we receive the Holy Spirit who helps our infirmities and aids our minds against the law that is in our members; it is realistic to encourage the baptized to sin no more.[22] God comes to us in baptism so that we may come to him and become like him. Baptism is the first step of initiation into the divinization process.

Once we have been given a new birth through baptism, we then obtain a new (spiritual) food through the Eucharist. Similar to Gregory of Nyssa, John of Damascus holds that the word of God is true and energizes; it is omnipotent in a manner which cannot be explained. "The bread of the table and the wine and water are supernaturally changed by the invocation (*epiklesis*) and presence of the Holy Spirit into the body and blood of Christ, and are not two but one and the same."[23] The power of the word in the *epiklesis* induces a change of the elements which is done through the Spirit in analogy to Jesus' becoming a human being. Bread and wine are united with the divine so that they have not just their earthly nature, but also divine. "The bread and the wine are not merely figures of the body and blood of Christ (God forbid!) but the deified body of the Lord itself." Though the term "*figura*" is rejected here, an actual transubstantiation is not asserted either. It is important to realize, however, that God is actually active and present in the Eucharist so that we receive remission of sins and assurance of life everlasting. The divine coal of the elements, to use John's phrase, consumes our sins and illumines our hearts "that we may be inflamed and deified by the participation of the divine fire." We are purified through the Eucharist and united to the body of Christ and to his Spirit and actually become the body of Christ.

When we consider the effects of the Eucharist, three points are especially noteworthy:

1. A danger: The Eucharist becomes an apotropaic tool through which we can protect ourselves against undesirable events. It shields us from all kinds of injury, purges us from uncleanness, and purifies "from diseases and all kinds of calamities."[24] This magical understanding of the eucharistic benefits, unacceptable as it is to us, may yet have some followers among Protestants. It should be noted, however, that the Seventh Ecumenical Council of 787 at Nicaea rejected the idea that after consecration the bread and wine are "pictures" of the body and blood of Christ. This served as a reminder that the image is worthless without the imaged from which this image gains its significance and under whose judgment the image stands. Whether the decisions of Nicaea could check the abuses in popular piety is, of course, a different question. Yet one should note that this important decision was the only dogmatic statement of the Eastern church on the Eucharist during the first millennium.

2. The communal aspect: Since we have communion with Christ and share in his flesh and in his divinity, "we have communion and are united with one another through it. For since we partake of one bread, we all become one body of Christ and one blood, and members of one another, being of one body with Christ." This aspect of the upbuilding of the community has deep biblical roots and, in recent times, has gained increased significance in Protestant quarters and is expressed with phrases such as "gathering around his table" or "altar fellowship."

3. Deification: This aspect is perhaps most foreign to the Western mind, though it should have evolved as a logical consequence from the Roman Catholic notion of transubstantiation. John of Damascus reminds us of the life-giving divine power of the sacrament when he says that the Eucharist becomes necessary for our existence, either for the future age or "for the preservation of our essence." The life-giving Spirit of the elements preserves us toward our eschatological

perfection and is essential to maintain our humanity. Only in union with the divine and empowered by it can we be truly human, fulfilling our function as the image of God.

When Eastern Christendom emphasized the notion of deification, it may have sensed something of the necessity of divine presence for remaining human. Of course, in the Eastern church the forgiveness of sin is still central to the Eucharist. But unlike Western Christendom, it also sensed the importance of the next step—union with Christ and the ensuing deification. The West, however, was so occupied with the immensity of human depravity that it hardly allowed for more than forgiveness, for cleansing and actual renewal.

The Western Emphasis on Divine Presence. When we now turn to the West and consult in the fourth century Bishop Ambrose of Milan, we notice at once the affinity of his deliberations to Eastern thought. When asked why it is that we receive the body of Christ though we do not see it, he responds: "This is not what nature made, but what the blessing consecrated, and the power of blessing is greater than that of nature, because by blessing nature itself is changed."[25] This means that actually a change takes place in the elements. Not "in, with, and under" the elements do we receive Christ, as Luther later asserted, but the matter has been changed while the form remains. Ambrose would not accept that we actually eat the body of Christ in a capernaitic manner, derived from a literal interpretation of John 6:53–58. He asserts: "In that sacrament is Christ, because it is the Body of Christ, it is therefore not bodily food but spiritual."[26] Bread and wine are received in a natural manner, while the body and blood, though received orally, are received in an incomprehensible, supernatural manner. Similar to this is also the line of thought that was later advocated by Lutheran orthodoxy,[27] of course, without admitting the notion of a change.

The North African bishop Augustine had too much background in Neoplatonic philosophy to pick up the idea of a change in the elements. For him the corporate benefits of the Eucharist were much more important. The Christian community is the body of Christ, and for its strengthening it receives the Spirit of Christ in the Eucharist since "the body of Christ cannot live but by the Spirit of

Christ."[28] Since the body of Christ is identified with the Christian community, Augustine can understand the sacramental presence of Christ in a much more "symbolic" way than did Ambrose. When we drink and eat that food it is therefore to dwell in Christ and to have Christ dwell in us. He can also state that "we are made better by participation of the Son, through the unity of His body and blood, which thing that eating and drinking signifies. We live then by Him, by eating Him; that is, by receiving Himself as the eternal life, which we did not have from ourselves."[29] Two points are noteworthy in Augustine's understanding of the Eucharist:

1. Augustine maintains a strict distinction between the outward sign and the inward reality. The unity of the body and blood is *signified* by the participation and presence of the Son in the eating and drinking. He can even talk of the figure (*figura*) of the body and blood of Christ. There is no doubt for Augustine that Christ is truly present in the sacrament since God is active in us through the sacred meal.

2. Since Christ is present in the Eucharist and we participate in his presence, the divinity of Christ makes us better persons and contributes to our sanctification. The divine presence draws us into him, making us more like him. As we have seen, this aspect of sanctification is especially important for the Eastern church.

We also note that Augustine does not speak of Christ's presence in human form, but in divine form only.[30] He has not yet conceptually developed the ubiquity of the person of Christ. While his human nature is necessarily confined to heaven, like a human body would be, his divine nature is everywhere and therefore also in the sacrament. As we shall see later, Calvin shared this conceptual shortcoming with Augustine, while Luther took the radical consequence of Christ's omnipresence to ensure the unity of the person. But the most important points in Augustine's system are not his metaphysical speculation. Augustine pays primary attention to what the Eucharist means and effects for us, namely, forgiveness of sins, participation in the benefits of Christ's salvific work and sanctification. This emphasis testifies to his study of Paul.

Noteworthy also is Augustine's understanding of the eucharistic sacrifice. He concentrates on the true sacrifice "which Christ alone offered on his altar. . . . This sacrifice is also commemorated by Christians, in this sacred offering and participation of the body and blood of Christ."[31] Sacrifice is a daily commemoration of Christ's sacrifice in the worshiping and self-giving community. The eucharistic sacrifice becomes a wellspring for the upbuilding of the body of Christ, namely the church. Thus there should be a daily sign of this sacrifice that the church, being Christ's body, learns to offer itself through Christ. These reflections, which largely build on the Fourth Gospel and on Paul, were rediscovered during the time of the Reformation and later at Vatican II. But they could not stem the tide of popular piety which urged for more tangible signs of the divine presence in the Eucharist.

Pope Gregory the Great, at the close of the sixth century, seems to have given in to that mood when he conceded that Christ, "is again immolated for us in the mystery of the holy sacrifice. Where His Body is eaten, there His Flesh is distributed among the people for their salvation";[32] and, "The souls of the dead sometimes beg to have Masses offered for them," since the holy sacrifice "brings great benefits to souls even after death, provided their sins can be pardoned in the life to come." The Eucharist has now become a repetition of Christ's original sacrifice on the cross; and it is performed to spare people from dangerous situations, to help the poor souls, and to benefit the living. This was the line of thought that continued on through many centuries, moderated on occasion by reforming movements.

Medieval Developments

In the early church the understanding of the Eucharist was characterized by the praise of the communing congregation toward God for his saving activity in Jesus Christ, the present Lord. In the medieval church the emphasis shifted to the gift that God gives to us in the Eucharist, his present Son. Then, of course, the question needed to be raised as to how he was present—through the change of the elements as Ambrose indicated or through outward signs of bread and wine. Theological reflection, which is never oblivious to popular piety, moved toward a more manifest presence of Christ through the change of the elements. This can be symptomatically seen in the two famous medieval controversies concerning the Eucharist. The first took place in the ninth century between the Benedictine monk Ratramnus and his abbot Paschasius Radbertus.

Ratramnus claimed that Christ's body was only figuratively present in the Eucharist, similar to some kind of overshadowing that reveals its contents under some sort of veil. He also insisted that what we call Christ's body and blood do indeed bear some resemblance to the body born to Mary. In both cases he talked about continuity between the two, but not physical identity. By distinguishing Christ's physical body from whatever is present in the sacrament, Ratramnus wanted to reject the idea that Christ was sacrificed anew each time the Mass was celebrated. He also wanted to refrain from the understanding of a capernaitic eating of the body of Christ. His opponent, Radbertus, however, insisted that though Christ had suffered once for all on the cross, "this offering is nevertheless repeated daily."[33] He also wanted to see an identity of the Jesus of history with Christ in the elements. But most important for him was the daily sacrifice to expiate daily sins. Thus the sacrifice of the Mass was urged much more earnestly than the reception of communion. Though at that time the literary dispute remained undecided, the Synod of Vercelli in 1050 condemned Ratramnus's writings against Radbertus, accusing them of containing false doctrine concerning the Eucharist. The reason for this belated action was that Berengar of Tours had set forth a doctrine of the Eucharist very similar to that of Ratramnus.

Very little of Berengar's writings have survived. Most of his thoughts must be gleaned from those who refuted him. In essence, he did not want to concede that the human physical body of Christ was identical with Christ's body in the Eucharist. This means the issue was basically the same as in the controversy between Radbertus and Ratramnus. Berengar was said to have claimed that the Eucharist "is not the true body of Christ nor his true blood, but some sort of figure and likeness."[34] Yet he was told in 1059 in Rome that "the bread and wine which are placed on the altar are, after consecration not only a sacrament, but the true body and blood of our Lord Jesus Christ."[35] Though forced to recant several times, Berengar never fully gave up following the Augustinian line that had also been pointed out by Ratramnus. Berengar attacked the identification of the Eucharist with the physical body of Christ, claiming, "the fathers proclaim that the body and blood are one thing and the sacraments of the body and blood are something else."[36]

For Berengar, to know Christ according to the flesh was to know him as subject to time and change; but the exalted Christ was no longer temporal or mutable, nor could his body come into being any more. But for most theologians of his time it was a stated fact that the bread was changed into the flesh of Christ, and this meant into that body that he received from his virgin mother. Of course, at ascension this flesh and body had been taken up into heaven. But Christ was not kept a prisoner there, unable to descend. Through the exaltation the flesh of Christ is present everywhere, wherever it pleases. If Christ so willed it his body could be present, completely and truly, in heaven and in the sacraments at one and the same time. This omnipresence, upon which Luther would later insist over against the Calvinists, still posed a problem to Berengar. The reason for this was not that he wanted to reject the real presence. He was repulsed, however, by the extravagant realism of Paschasius, interpreted through gross stories about the change of the elements into a body laying on the altar or into a piece of flesh. Some of these stories and legends may have come from the East and were, for instance, popularized by Gregory the Great.[37] Thus Berengar defiantly rejected the idea that the elements had undergone a transformation and instead wanted to affirm a continuity between Christ and the elements on the altar. "As Saul of Tarsus was changed into Paul the apostle by remaining what he was and yet becoming something else, so it was with the elements in the Sacrament."[38]

We note that Berengar liberally used the word "change" with reference to the elements. But for him wine and bread were not changed to be replaced by the body and blood of Christ while retaining all the qualities of bread and wine as his opponents would have it. For him they remained what they were and were changed into something else in addition. "I grant," he confessed, "that the bread and wine of the altar become, after consecration, according to the Scriptures, the body and blood of Christ, and so I can concede that after consecration the *very* bread and wine become for faith and understanding (*fidei et intellectui*), the true body and blood of

Christ, yet not materially but spiritually, not through absorption but addition."[39]

Berengar and his followers could not convince the majority of scholars nor the populace in their attempt to explain the miracle of the eucharistic change. The church insisted that it was indeed a true and mystical change that took place through the consecration. Before the consecration the bread set forth on the Lord's Table was nothing but bread; but in the consecration, by the ineffable power of the Divinity, the nature and substance of the bread were converted into the nature and substance of the flesh of Christ. Only the outward appearance of the elements remained. One could no longer speak of the "figure" (*figura*) of the divine presence but of the substance of Christ's body and blood over against the accidents of bread and wine. Soon the church arrived at a definite statement of the doctrine of the real presence, saying: "The priest himself is the sacrifice, Jesus Christ, whose body and blood are truly contained in the sacrament of the altar under the species of bread and wine; the bread (changed) into His body by the divine power of transubstantiation, and the wine into the blood."[40] This doctrine of transubstantiation, decreed at the Fourth Lateran Council in 1215 was reaffirmed in 1551 at the Council of Trent against the Protestant "heresies." Until very recently it has been a major point of difference between the Roman Catholic Church and most Protestant denominations.

The doctrine of transubstantiation led to a reduction of the threefold understanding of the body of Christ—that is, physical, sacramental, and ecclesial—to a twofold by collapsing the physical and the sacramental into one. Yet the Lateran Council did not create a uniform interpretation of the doctrine of transubstantiation. For instance, one could still distinguish between the faith in the real presence of Christ and the theory of the mode of this presence. One theory was that of consubstantiation. It claimed that the conversion did not lead to a real change of the substance of bread and wine but added to it the substance of body and blood. Another theory was that of annihilation or of substitution. Here the substance of bread and wine was annihilated while its accidents (i.e., outward appearance) remained. It was then substituted by the substance of body and blood under the accidents of bread and wine. Again this would not mean a real change but a temporal succession. While Thomas Aquinas and Bonaventure thought the theory of consubstantiation to be heretical, John Duns Scotus did not feel it to be excluded through Scripture, and William of Occam thought the coexistence of the body of Christ together with the substance of the bread not only possible but even more convincing than other theories.

The more attention the church paid to the real personal presence of the Lord in the eucharistic elements, the more his actual salvific work receded into the background. It was also less necessary to commune with both bread and wine than with one element (bread). This emerging custom of communing with bread only was furthered by the fear of spilling the wine (blood) and also by the scarcity of wine in northern countries. The main aspect of the Eucharist for the laity was fear and reverence. This soon led to the adoration of the elements, especially the body, in the elevation at the altar and in the sacramental processions which finally ensued in the feast of Corpus Christi. The Eucharist was less and less understood as nourishment on the way to eternity, and more as the presence of the eternal in the midst of a transitory world. Thus a static notion of the Eucharist prevailed. The increase in adoration also made it less urgent to commune regularly and frequently. It was safer simply to adore the elements. "The laity went once, the very pious twice to four times a year, the clergy once a month or even once a week." Within monastic orders "the lay brothers and lay sisters were not permitted to take Communion as often as the clergy and the choir-sisters. It would have been considered presumptuous if they had aspired to equality."[41]

The Emphasis of the Reformation

During the time of the Reformation every conceivable position concerning the Eucharist emerged, from the extreme position of a rejection of visible signs (Enthusiasts) to the insistence upon the centrality of the real presence (Lutherans). Yet the main force of the Reformation did not want to espouse new doctrines of the Eucharist but simply wanted to reject certain abuses. They insisted on communion under bread and wine, on the absolute priority of communion of the elements over against their adoration, and on the singular nonrepeatable sacrifice of Christ on the cross for all people. Beyond these common points we can discern basically three positions.

The Communal Meal. The Anabaptist tradition neither recognizes a clergy nor sacraments. Yet we encounter a common supper which focuses on historical continuity with the last supper and with Christ's sacrifice on the cross. In a letter of Konrad Grebel and his brethren to Thomas Müntzer (1524) we get some insight into Anabaptist theology.[42] Concerning the last supper, Grebel lists altogether sixteen points: (1) The common supper was instituted by Christ. (2) Only the words of institution according to Matthew 26, Mark 14, Luke 22, or 1 Corinthians 11 shall be used. (3) Servants from the congregation should read aloud one of these versions. (4) The words of institution denote a common meal and not a consecration of the elements. (5) Plain bread and (6) common drinking vessels are to be used. (7) While the bread is only bread, it is in faith the body of Christ and the joining to one body of Christ and the brethren. Thus one must eat it in spirit and in love. (8) Though it is only bread it should be taken with gladness, provided that such is preceded by faith and brotherly love. (9) Someone who does not live in brotherly love eats it to his condemnation. He does not discern it from other meals and defiles the inner bond of love and the outward sign of bread. (10) The Supper would also remind him of the body and blood of Christ, the covenant on the cross, and of his willingness to live and suffer for the sake of Christ and the brethren. (11) The Supper is a communal sign and not a Mass or a sacrament. One should not administer or receive it alone. (12) It should not be celebrated in "temples." (13) It should be celebrated frequently. (14) It should not be celebrated without applying the rule of Christ (Matt. 18:15–18), that is, without brotherly admonition and forgiveness. (15) It should be administered without clergical garb, vestments, singing, or any other additions. (16) Though Christ celebrated it at night, one can celebrate it at any time of the day.

Grebel's recommendations show a strong emphasis on original simplicity and on the communal aspect. While the presence of Christ in the elements is still maintained, it is at most a spiritual presence. In Michael Sattler's *Schleitheim Confession* of 1527, still influential today in Anabaptist (Mennonite) quarters, the reference to Christ's presence is completely missing. The Supper is strictly a memorial meal. Those who have dedicated themselves to Christ and are united as his body break the bread and drink the wine to remember the broken body and the shed blood. At the same time they demonstrate their break with the world and its prince, the devil:

> All those who desire to break the one bread in remembrance of the broken body of Christ and all those who wish to drink of one drink in remembrance of the shed blood of Christ, they must beforehand be united in the one body of Christ, that is the congregation of God, whose head is Christ, and that by baptism. For as Paul indicates, we cannot be partakers at the same time of the table of the Lord and the table of devils. Nor can we at the same time partake and drink of the cup of the Lord and the cup of devils. That is: all those who have fellowship with the dead works of darkness have no part in the light. Thus all who follow the devil and the world have no part with those who have been called out of the world unto God. All those who lie in evil have no part in the good.
>
> So it shall and must be, that whoever does not share the calling of the one God to one faith, to one baptism, to one spirit, to one body together with all the children of God, may not be made one loaf together with them, as must be true if one wishes truly to break bread according to the command of Christ.[43]

We hear no longer of a communion with Christ in the Lord's Supper, but just a communion with the brethren who participate in the Supper. In a literal sense the Supper has become a fellowship meal. With this interpretation the Anabaptists moved far away from the kind of understanding which they first encountered in Zwingli's Zurich. When they discovered that, for their taste, Zwingli did not move quickly and far enough in his reforms, they broke with him and formed their own movement.

Between Memorial and Gift. The Reformed tradition is shaped in its origin principally by two persons, Ulrich Zwingli and John Calvin. *Ulrich Zwingli* had learned much from both Erasmus and Luther. In the explanation of thesis 18 of his *67 Schlussreden* ("theses"; 1523) he openly confessed his affinity to Luther and yet his independence from him: "When Luther preaches Christ, he does exactly the same as I do, though, God be praised, through him innumerably more people are led to God than through me or any other."[44] He emphasized that he had called the celebration of the body and blood of Christ a memorial (*Wiedergedächtnis*) of Christ's suffering before he had ever heard Luther's name. "And Luther called the body and blood of Christ a will (*Testament*). Both terms are proper and come from the mouth of Christ." The one denotes the essence, the other the practice. "When one eats and drinks one does not offer a sacrifice, but remembers and renews what Christ had once done." At this point Zwingli emphasized Christ's singular and unrepeatable sacrifice, but did not yet polemicize against Luther's insistence on Christ's real presence.

When Zwingli acknowledges that Luther talks about the essence while he talks about practice, this is not yet a point of controversy. Soon after, however, he emphasized the personal faith as a condition for receiving the Eucharist. One partakes of the Eucharist only if one has faith. When we hear that bread and wine are consumed in vain "if the one who eats does not strongly believe that this is only nourishment for the soul; if he is certain that the body of Christ given and slaughtered for us has freed us from all tyranny of the devil, sin, and death,"[45] a further step has been taken. Zwingli has relativized the external action of the Eucharist. He also no longer sees a connection between the elements of the Eucharist and what Christ has wrought with his body and blood.

Through the influence of the Dutch lawyer Cornelius Honius, Zwingli finally became convinced that the "is" in the words of the institution actually meant "signifies." Honius also declared that Christ came into flesh only once. Thus he could never be again in the bread. After Zwingli became familiar with the ideas of Honius (1524), he rejected the character of the Eucharist as a gift and Christ's real presence. Decisive for him became the action of the faithful participants and of the congregation. In his *De vera et falsa religione Commentarius* ((*Commentary on the true and false religion*, 1524/25), he avoided mention of the term "sacrament." A sacrament cannot mediate grace. It can only be an initiation or a public certification. The Eucharist is a commemoration through which those who steadfastly believe that they are reconciled through Christ's death and blood proclaim his life-giving death. Real presence and transubstantiation are indiscriminately rejected. Those who think they eat the body of Christ are called cannibals or meat eaters. Those, however, who symbolically eat the bread of Christ's body are summoned to live according to Christ's command, since he has given them an example. For Zwingli the Lord's Supper has become a memorial meal, a confessional meal, and a community meal. We remember Christ's saving action, we proclaim his salvational death, and are strengthened in brotherly love.

When we now touch on *John Calvin* we must realize that to this day there is no consensus on his exact understanding of the Lord's Supper.[46] He reveals Augustinian thought when he distinguished in the sacrament between word and sign. In contrast to Zwingli he also emphasizes the character of the sacrament as a gift. As with Zwingli he is convinced that a sacrament, to be efficacious, must be received in faith. Its task is to strengthen our faith. In his *Institutes of the Christian Religion* he provides a comprehensive treatment of the Eucharist. He clearly demonstrates its relationship to baptism when he says: "God has received us, once for all, into his family . . . he has willed by giving his pledge, to assure us of this continuing liberality. To this end, therefore, he has . . . given to his church another sacrament, that is, a spiritual banquet, wherein Christ attests himself to be the life-giving bread, upon which our souls feed unto true and blessed immortality (John 6:51)."[47]

"Godly souls can gather great assurance and delight from this Sacrament; in it they have a witness of our growth into one body with Christ such that whatever is his may be called ours."[48] Important here are the benefits of the Eucharist, namely that we participate in divine immortality. Once Calvin has laid his theological foundation of the Eucharist, he discusses the downgrading of the Eucharist by Zwingli and his followers and its overestimation by Luther and his disciples. Then he provides his own interpretation of the words of institution, deals with christological issues, the use by believers and the unworthy, and finally considers the proper eucharistic practice. In conclusion he devotes a special chapter to the Roman Mass.

When Calvin comes to the words of the institution he asserts that a word always needs interpretation. Since the word "is" can hardly mean "to be equivalent," it cannot be taken literally. Yet mere symbolism does not suffice either. To ascertain the true humanity of Christ, Calvin teaches that Christ sits after his ascension at the right hand of God. But the faithful receive Christ and his heavenly body and blood while eating the Supper. Though he is not bodily present among the faithful, they (i.e., their souls) are united with him through the power of the Spirit. Thus Calvin teaches a spiritual presence of Christ. "When we see wine set forth as a symbol of blood, we must reflect on the benefits which wine imparts to the body, and so realize that the same are spiritually imparted to us by Christ's blood. These benefits are to nourish, refresh, strengthen, and gladden."[49] The sacrament therefore affects the faithful spiritually. Consequently Calvin excludes the reception of Christ by the unworthy. Weak as it may be, there must always be some faith present to reap the benefits. Although Christ's body is also offered to the unworthy they receive only bread and wine. For the faithful, however, the Holy Spirit makes present Christ's body so that they participate in its benefits.

Finally Calvin strongly recommends frequent celebration of the Eucharist. He claims that the custom of celebrating the Eucharist only once a year is an invention of the devil.[50] A more frequent celebration strengthens the faith of the Christians. And we also hear that the Eucharist will nourish mutual love and fellowship; it has a communal aspect and binds the community together as the body of Christ. It also invigorates the individual Christian in the hope of immortality.

In contrast to Zwingli, Calvin's emphasis in his understanding of the Eucharist is on the primacy of God's action. God offers us his gift, the salvational benefits of Christ's death, and asks us to receive them. Yet Calvin does not totally exclude our own cooperation.

Christ's Real Presence. The Lutheran tradition is largely shaped through Martin Luther and his close collaborator, Philip Melanchthon. Beyond the insistence upon Christ's real presence, Lutherans have refrained from assertions about the mode of Christ's presence.

Nor were they as explicit as the Reformed theologians in developing a theory of the communion with Christ. Only in the later struggles, which ensued in Lutheran orthodoxy, was more specificity attained as to the reception of Christ in the Eucharist.

There was never any doubt for *Martin Luther* that Christ was truly present in the Eucharist. Similar to Zwingli, Luther initially emphasized the communion aspect of the Supper very strongly. Yet in contrast to Zwingli, he pointed to the communion between Christ and the believer and not just to that among the believers. So he could state: "The significance or effect of this sacrament is fellowship of all the saints. From this it derives its common name *synaxis* or *communio*, that is, fellowship. And the Latin *communicare* . . . means to take part in this fellowship. Hence it is that Christ and all the saints are one spiritual body."[51] Christ is present in the Supper offering us forgiveness of sins and comforting us in temptation. In this first period of reflection on the Lord's Supper (1518/19) Luther found the Mass to be destructive of communion, since there was so much works-righteousness connected with it.[52] He also attacked the concept of an *opus operatum*, that is, the idea that the performance of the sacrament itself would have saving value.[53] But he still stayed within traditional boundaries and accepted the idea of a change or of the transubstantiation of the elements.[54] Similar to Calvin, he still defined the Lord's Supper as an outward sign that had inner and spiritual significance.[55] While this is also in line with the Augustinian tradition, he added faith as a third moment to sign and significance which ties both together and makes them fruitful.

In his second phase, beginning in 1520, his starting point was no longer a definition of a sacrament but the exegesis of the words of the institution. This point of departure remained constant for him in his disputes with various groups of the Reformation and in his attack on the Roman Mass. Luther now regards the words of the institution to form the main part of the Mass.[56] Their promissory character gained special prominence for him. Realizing that Christ instituted the Supper just before his death as his last will (testament), Luther declared: "And so that little word 'testament' [RSV: covenant] is a short summary of all God's wonders and grace, fulfilled in Christ."[57] When Luther called the Mass "a testament and sacrament," that is,

"God's word or promise, together with a sacred sign, the bread and the wine under which Christ's flesh and blood are truly present,"[58] we notice that he no longer maintained the concept of an actual transubstantiation. The unifying character of the Lord's Supper, which had been important to him before, loses emphasis. Decisive is the communion of the individual believer with Jesus Christ. The existential significance, that is, the "for me," attains more prominence. Yet the Eucharist is still understood to be given by Christ that we may be united and that this unification may become a practice of our whole life.[59]

In the Babylonian Captivity of the Church (1520) Luther's own understanding of the Eucharist was sufficiently clarified and distinctive from the Roman tradition so that he heavily attacked its prevailing teaching and practice on three points: (1) the first captivity of the church consists in refusing the chalice to the laity.[60] This goes against Christ's words of institution. We should also keep in mind that "the sacrament is not for the priests but for all and the priests are not masters but servants." (2) The second captivity is found in the idea of transubstantiation. This doctrine is a "figment of the human mind, for it rests neither on the Scriptures nor on reason."[61] (3) The third captivity concerns the idea that the Eucharist is a good work and a sacrifice. It is repulsive for Luther to think that we should give anything to God since we are actually the recipients.[62] We should accept his promises and administer the sacrament instead of attempting to sacrifice the sacrifice. This third point is again forcefully addressed in the Smalcald Articles where Luther declared: "The Mass is and can be nothing else than a human work, even a work of evil scoundrels (as the canon and all the books on the subject declare), for by means of the Mass men try to reconcile themselves and others to God and obtain and merit grace and the forgiveness of sins."[63] With this attack the prevailing practice and understanding of the Eucharist was declared invalid and the break with Rome on the Eucharist was the logical consequence. It should be pointed out, however, that Luther put much more weight on the false understanding of the Mass as a work and a sacrifice, while he was more lenient on the issue of communion under bread and wine.[64]

From now on the emphasis on the real presence gained more and more significance for Luther. This was largely due to the emerging disputes with the Enthusiasts and Zwingli. Luther had received a letter from Honius, perhaps because he believed that Luther too understood the Eucharist as a down payment to which a promise had been added. In this letter Honius advanced a symbolic interpretation of the words of institution. Yet in contrast to Zwingli, who was decidedly influenced by this letter, Luther attacked Honius's new interpretation in 1523 with the remark:

> For if we permit such violence to be done in one passage, that without any basis in Scripture a person can say the word "is" means the same as the word "signifies," then it would be impossible to stop it in any other passage. The entire Scripture would be nullified, since there would be no good reason why such violence should be valid in one passage but not in all passages. In that case one could say: That Mary is a virgin and the mother of God is equivalent to saying that Mary signifies a virgin and the mother of God. Likewise: Christ is God and man; that is, Christ signifies God and man.[65]

This response shows that in Luther's insistence on a "literal" interpretation of the word "is" more was at stake than just the words of the institution. It was a hermeneutical key that assured the validity and objectivity of the biblical statements. If he allowed a symbolic (signifying) or allegorical interpretation, Luther was afraid that there would be no end of bending the words according to one's own preference. Luther was reacting here also to the often grotesque and exaggerated symbolism of his time. But his literal stance made a clash with Zwingli inevitable. This was compounded by the fact that as early as 1520 Luther had declared that John 6 had nothing whatsoever to do with the Eucharist.[66] But this passage played a prominent role for Zwingli who used it to assert his symbolic understanding of the Lord's presence. Calvin too referred to it quite frequently.

It was only a matter of time therefore, until Luther would clash with Zwingli who served as the other influential figure of the nascent Reformation. For Luther real presence did not only mean the presence of the person of Christ but the presence of his sacrificed and exalted body and blood. To assert this kind of real presence convincingly, Luther developed the theory of ubiquity. He wanted to answer the question of how, after his ascension, Christ could be at a certain place in heaven and at the same time be at many places according to his human nature. In 1526 he asserted the ubiquity of Christ for the first time: "We believe that Christ, according to his human nature, is put over all creatures and fills all things . . . not only according to his divine nature, but also according to his human nature, he is a lord of all things, has all things in his hand, and is present everywhere."[67] This ubiquity of Christ's divine and human natures was possible through the *communicatio idiomatum* ("exchange of properties") through which the human nature could participate in the properties of the divine nature and vice versa. Since Christ is present everywhere, his presence in the Eucharist is the disclosure of his general presence to strengthen the faithful and fortify their faith.

With these considerations Luther did not want to develop a theory of Christ's presence in the Eucharist. On the contrary, he was not interested in such a theory. Yet he wanted to make sure that he could communicate the whole meaning of the words of institution. Christ is really present in his whole person in the elements. Luther even spoke of a "flesh-bread or a body-bread" indicating the unity of the elements with the whole Christ.[68] Zwingli, on the other hand, understood the words of institution differently and, consequently, was much less interested in Christ's bodily presence. By calling the Eucharist a memorial meal (*Wiedergedächtnis*) he did not just want to remember it as something that had occurred long ago. For him it was something that still had significance for the present. Since Christ had once and for all effected our salvation, Zwingli did not want to leave the impression that such an act could be repeated in the Eucharist. Yet still the congregation became for him the agent actually acting in the Eucharist appropriating for themselves Christ's sacrifice. Zwingli also did not want to bring the two natures of Christ as closely together as Luther. He only admitted a spiritual presence of Christ in the Eucharist according to his divine nature, but not a presence according to the divine and human natures as Luther had done.[69]

It is clear that such differences could not be bridged, though political authorities pushed for an agreement for the sake of a common alliance among the major forces of the Reformation. While neither party was willing to give up its respective position at the Marburg Colloquy (1529), both made considerable concessions. In Article 15 both agreed that the Mass is not a work through which one could obtain grace for someone else. Zwingli then conceded to Luther that "the sacrament of the altar is a sacrament of the true body and blood of Christ," while Luther conceded to Zwingli that "the spiritual usage of this same body and blood is especially necessary for every Christian."[70] Finally Zwingli admitted that as with the word, the Holy Spirit moves the weak conscience toward faith in the Eucharist. Zwingli thereby admitted the character of the Eucharist as a gift through which grace is mediated. He also affirmed its sacramental nature. Luther, on the other hand, conceded its spiritual usage. But both failed to agree that "the true body and blood of Christ is bodily present in bread and wine." Yet they hoped that this issue would also be settled at some later date. This was the limit to which either side was able to move at that time.

When *Philip Melanchthon* wrote the Augsburg Confession in 1530 he took the unresolved issue from Marburg, affirmed Christ's real presence, and made this the center of the Lutheran position on the Eucharist, saying: "It is taught among us that the true body and blood of Christ are really present in the Supper of our Lord under the form of bread and wine and are there distributed and received. The contrary doctrine is therefore rejected."[71] The hope for a settlement of this one issue (bodily presence) was gone. Yet the Latin version of Article 10 of the Augsburg Confession did not state a *manducatio oralis* ("an oral eating of body and blood"), and left open the possibility of a *manducatio spiritualis* ("spiritual eating"), a version which would have been much more amenable to the Reformed side. In the Apology of the Augsburg Confession Melanchthon took an unexpected step. In his attempt to move as closely as possible to the Roman side he asserted with a quote from an eleventh-century writer that "the bread is not merely a figure but is truly changed into flesh."[72] But he never really intended to assert the doctrine of transubstantiation. On the contrary, the longer he studied the ancient theologians the more skeptical he grew of Luther's "merging" of the elements with the body and blood of Christ. When Luther told him in preparation for a 1534 meeting with Bucer: "This is our statement: The body is with the bread, so that whatever motion or action the bread makes the body of Christ makes too,"[73] Melanchthon felt that he was only a "messenger of an alien statement."[74]

According to Melanchthon, we hear in a statement of 1555, "there is no change of the substance of the bread," as the Romans would want.[75] "With bread and wine the son of God is truly and essentially present." But once the sacramental use has ceased it is plain bread. The real presence of Christ, in which Melanchthon always believed, is reserved for the sacramental use of the elements. Thus he also arrived at a variation of Article 10 of the Augsburg Confession saying that: "Concerning the Lord's Supper it is taught that the body and blood of Christ are truly offered and received with bread and wine."[76] Of course, this statement did not exactly reflect Luther's insistence that "in" the elements are Christ's body and blood. But it may reflect a more biblical concept of a "symbolic realism," and also a possibility of a reconciliation with the Reformed side. Yet at that time both sides were too eager to justify their own positions. They were not yet ready to go back to the biblical foundations of the Eucharist and reflect together on its actual meaning.

THE MEANING OF THE LORD'S SUPPER FOR TODAY

The central sacrament of the Christians that should unite all faithful has been the source of division and separation for many centuries. In our historical survey we mentioned at least five groups—Anabaptists, Lutherans, Calvinists, Roman Catholics, and Eastern Orthodox—all of which refuse to each other, in varying degrees, altar fellowship. Can we really blame people when they state that the history of the Eucharist is "the history of suffering" and "one of the most unpleasant parts of the history of dogma."[77]

A Convergence of Traditions

Particularly after Vatican II and the formation of vigorous confessional families, we notice a convergence of traditions that leaves us with the hope that the sacrament of unity may indeed one day be expressive of the unity we share as children of God and brothers and sisters of Christ. This move forward to a common understanding of the Eucharist was furthered considerably by two phenomena: (1) a growing awareness that one's own position on the Eucharist is in part historically conditioned by the special circumstances under which this position first emerged; and (2) a growing willingness to listen together to the biblical documents that decidedly influenced our historically developed positions.

Perhaps the Leuenberg Agreement of the European Churches of the Reformation of 1973 captured this new mood correctly when it observed that many of the stereotypes no longer hold as one reconsiders and reinterprets one's own history and the history of other denominations, and as biblical exegesis leads to deeper insight. For instance, Calvin could not effectively relate the divine omnipresence of Christ through the Spirit with Christ's presence at the right hand of the Father. Since this separation also violated the unity of the person of Christ, the question emerges whether this dichotomy must be maintained today. Certainly the Heidelberg Catechism still tells us that "although he [Christ] is in heaven and we are on earth, we are nevertheless flesh of his flesh and bone of his bone, always living and being governed by one Spirit, as the members of our bodies are governed by one soul."[78] A contemporary commentator suggests that this statement reflects "a sacramental realism" and does not mean that Christ is present only symbolically in and with the elements. Reformed theologians even assert that we "eat the crucified body of Christ" and we drink "his shed blood."

We realize that both the Reformed tradition and the Lutherans emphasize the real presence. But for Lutherans this emphasis has not been coupled with an equal specificity concerning the circumstances of his presence. They do not reflect on the Holy Spirit as the mediator of the real presence nor on how the presence in heaven differs from that in the Lord's Supper. Their official documents (CA 10!) show a remarkable restraint, if not a total lack of interest in discussing the mode of his presence. Here the Roman Catholic tradition shows the other side of the spectrum.

After long struggles the Roman Catholic Church became more and more explicit of the exact mode of Christ's presence in the

Eucharist and finally accepted a theory of transubstantiation. Yet today, when the influence of scholastic philosophy (with the aid of which this theory was developed) is waning, there is a renewed discussion of what this theory actually means. Basically it attempts to assert that God acts in the Eucharist, effecting a change in the elements. But it is not a rationalistic attempt to explain the mystery of Christ's presence in the elements.[79] Similar to the Reformed and the Lutheran assertions concerning the real presence, it shows the limits of a single term or conceptual framework in adequately exploring the mystery of Christ's presence. We even could make the same claim for the Eastern Orthodox tradition. There, too, the terms "change," "transubstantiation," and "re-creation" indicate that the elements of bread and wine are inseparably united with the body and blood of Christ without arriving at a final concept. This means that with different conceptual tools the presence of Christ in his sacrament is asserted.

Yet does it really make sense to identify the body and blood of Jesus of Nazareth with "the heavenly body and blood" of Jesus Christ that we might receive in the Eucharist? If Jesus was resurrected to a new being, into a new body, then we should not talk about corporeal identity—it is no longer the old body, not even under the disguise of the new—but rather about personal identity.[80] As Paul reminded us, "flesh and blood cannot inherit the kingdom of God" (1 Cor. 15:50), but only a new being. Luther was right when he objected to Zwingli's spiritualism in which he rejected the sacramental realism of Christ's actual presence by asserting against Luther: "The flesh is of no avail." Yet Luther himself attempted to alleviate Zwingli's fear of a crassly corporeal presence of Christ when he replied to Zwingli: "If Christ's flesh is eaten, nothing but spirit comes of it, for it is a spiritual flesh and does not let itself be transformed, but transforms the person who eats it and gives him the Spirit."[81] The one who gives the Spirit is the person of Christ whose human body suffered for our sake. The gift of the Lord's Supper is not a supernatural substance that we could eat and drink sacramentally, such as in mystery cults; but it is received in and with drinking ordinary wine and eating ordinary bread. Jesus Christ gives *himself* truly to us in his sacrifice and therewith gathers and strengthens the Christian community as his living body.

We should also remember that it is Christ who is present in and with the elements. Since Christ is equal with God, any comprehensive theory of his presence would encounter difficulties similar to those the early church encountered in its attempts to assert rationally how the divine and the human "aspects" in Christ are related to each other. After many and often violent discussions the church finally reached the significant insight: We know and confess that Christ is truly human and truly divine. Yet we are unable to assert how to relate both aspects. We only know how they cannot be related. Similarly, in fully ascertaining Christ's personal presence in and with the Lord's Supper, we must admit that he is truly present. But none of the prevalent denominational theories completely suffices as a description of this presence. It is as difficult to reject entirely consubstantiation as being incomplete, as it is to eliminate transubstantiation as being heretical. Perhaps the Council of Trent should have heeded more its own insight when it declared that the sacramental presence is such that "we can scarcely express it in words, yet we can, however, by our understanding illuminated by faith, conceive it to be possible for God, and which we ought most steadfastly to believe."[82] Acknowledging our conceptual limitations, we should nevertheless continually endeavor to press for the most intellectually satisfying and biblically sound theory of his presence unless we want to shroud our affirmation of Christ's presence with undue mystery.

The Roman Catholic emphasis on the manifest sacramental presence of Christ has engendered several other customs. For instance, Roman Catholics have developed very distinct procedures about what to do with the undistributed bread and wine. The wine is always consumed by the presiding priest, while the usage of the consecrated host for the communion of the sick and shut-ins, as advocated again by Vatican II, has an ancient tradition. In contrast the Lutherans are often uncertain about what to do with the undistributed elements.[83] They often use the bread again for the next Eucharist thus having it consecrated once more, while pouring the wine on the ground or even down the drain. The more reverential handling of the consecrated elements, while familiar to Luther himself, would certainly be worthy of serious contemplation by his followers. But the Roman Catholics go beyond basic piety in the feast of Corpus Christi and the adoration of the host. Yet today they rediscover too that adoration is not the first and original purpose of the host, as one might conclude by just observing their reverence for the consecrated elements, but the orientation toward communion. Though now the Roman Catholic Church seems to subordinate more the adorational processional practices to the liturgy of the Mass, it still has not been sufficiently clarified that the consecrated elements lose their significance outside the communion with the Lord.

Another point of contention is the relation between the preached word and sacrament. The churches of the Reformation placed so much emphasis on the preached word that the Eucharist often appeared as a mere appendage to the service of the word and was only occasionally celebrated. As the *Lutheran Book of Worship* shows, there is a significant reversal of this unbiblical trend as Lutherans rediscover the necessary bond between proclamation and sacrament, celebrating the Eucharist as the main service. In the Roman Catholic Church, however, the Mass has gained so much attention in the past that the proclamation of the word was sorely neglected. Again, since Vatican II this trend has been reversed, especially through the "rediscovery of the Bible" and the increased emphasis on the use of the vernacular. Now there is growing awareness in Roman Catholic quarters too, that a service of the word (without the Eucharist) is also a complete and valid service.

With the Roman Catholic elevation of the Eucharist as the manifestation of the divine, its celebration became such a priestly affair that the laity need not even be present. Lutherans always objected to *Winkelmessen* ("Eucharists in the corner") which were solely performed and attended by a priest. Today, however, the Roman Catholic Church is rediscovering the communal dimension of the Eucharist and is placing more emphasis on it. Priests are encouraged to celebrate the Eucharist together in those instances where no lay people are present. So we hear from Vatican II that "priests are strongly urged to celebrate Mass every day, for even if the faithful are unable to be present, it is an act of Christ and the Church."[84] While the Roman Catholic Church has recognized that Mass is not a private thing and encourages Mass with other faithful being present, it still considers Mass offered in private a distinct possibility. Yet then it is understood as an act of Christ and the church and therefore not a private act. Though the public dimension of the

Eucharist is given more emphasis we wonder whether this is sufficient to satisfy its constituent communal aspect.

Another point of longstanding contention is the Roman Catholic practice of reserving the chalice for the priest. Underlying this practice is the fear that by communing the laity with the chalice wine might be spilled and therefore the blood of Christ be desecrated. While it is true that the whole Christ is fully present in each of the two elements (bread and wine), Protestants are rightly concerned with the perfection and completeness of the sacramental symbol in accordance with its institution. Roman Catholics today agree that the sacramental sign is more perfect and more complete if communion is given under both forms than under one form only. Consequently the offering of the chalice to laypersons has recently been permitted in a number of special cases. Yet this is still a far cry from Luther's demand that the chalice be given to all lay people who commune. If the sacrament is really as important for salvation as Roman Catholics say it is, it should not be given to the laity in a "diminished" form, unless we would conclude that they are less in need of it than the priests. Yet the widespread Protestant custom of communing with individual cups hardly symbolizes the original communal aspect of the meal. When the common cup is used, Roman Catholics rightly object that it has often aesthetically unpleasing side effects, for instance, when an oily film develops on the surface of the wine or when the danger arises that colds are passed on with the common cup. While the first objection could be alleviated by using a second and third cup so that none is used for too many people, the second objection could be eliminated by some people refraining from the common cup if they might pass on colds or other contagious diseases.

Finally one more point of contention and convergence ought to be mentioned, the idea that the Mass could be celebrated on behalf of the dead. This custom has had a long tradition in the Roman Catholic Church. The Augsburg Confession explicitly condemned the idea that Mass could be an atonement for the living and the dead, an idea which it saw originating from the opinion "that Christ had by this passion made satisfaction for original sin and had instituted the Mass in which an oblation should be made for daily sins, mortal and venial."[85] We noted that the Council of Trent did not leave out completely a reflection upon the attitude of the participant of the Eucharist. Thus the popular notion that certain forms of Mass or Mass series would have an unfailing effect for the redemption of a soul was rejected there too. But if the Eucharist makes present the sacrifice on the cross, then this would also allow the possibility of supplication for the dead. It is interesting at least that the contemporary Lutheran adult catechism in Germany states: "In its prayers the community intercedes with God for the deceased asking him for forgiveness for sins, acceptance by God, and the granting of eternal Life."[86] While Roman Catholics would side with Lutherans to say that the Mass is no means of attempting to change the lot of the deceased through one's own efforts, it is certainly within the realm of biblical freedom to ask God to consider, in his mercy, the eternal destiny of our loved ones, both living and dead. Again we notice a growing together of the two traditions that may, however, in popular piety still differ considerably.

Almost parenthetically we should also mention here the longstanding tradition in Eastern Orthodoxy whereby the infant moves from baptism to confirmation and to communion, all being part of the initiation rite. This tradition is also gaining consideration among some Lutherans. Indeed, if baptism is the full initiation, then communion could follow immediately. The same could be argued for other sacraments such as ordination or marriage. Luther himself stated that through baptism one is already a priest, a bishop, and a pope. But he also demanded proper education and reception of a call before one could assume the priestly office. Full initiation does not imply that one should assume all privileges of full membership in the visible church. For instance, one does not allow infants to vote at congregational meetings, although theologically we could hardly bar them from exercising this right. Baptism is also much more than an initiation rite. There is the primacy of God's grace, God's yes to us sinners; and there is the human response, the asking for baptism and the growing up in faith. As Luther rightly recognized, baptism is not a one-time occasion but a lifelong process. Communion is then not a logical next step to be taken as soon as possible after baptism, but a different way in which God discloses himself to us in his grace and in which his grace can be appropriated by us.

Since infant communion was not mentioned until the middle of the third century one might want to reject it with the argument that its prominence stems from the emergence of the prevalent practice of infant baptism, when missionary adult baptism became more the exception than the rule. But why did the Western church then finally abandon infant communion and retain infant baptism? Perhaps the reason was not only an increasing reverence for the Sacrament of the Altar, but also the realization that as one progresses in life different aspects of God's gracious self-disclosure should be made available. We should also ask the Eastern churches why they do not insist that infants commune as often as do adults. Perhaps in their tradition the "natural move from the font to the altar" is more symbolic than real. While we cannot, on theological grounds, exclude Christian children from communion, ordination, or any other participation among the faithful, we should at least consider whether it is not sound practice to provide certain sacraments at certain points of life as helpful aids toward the goal of sanctification. The move toward a more flexible communion age seems to point in the right direction. It removes a legal barrier and instead establishes a guideline for Christian life and growth. Similarly, the practice in many churches of bringing children to the altar to be blessed while their parents receive communion indicates that children too are welcome at the Table of the Lord to be blessed by his presence, which is not confined to the elements but occurs in word and sacrament.

The Visible Presence of Divine Grace

Exciting and significant as such convergence toward a common understanding of the Eucharist among major Christian denominations may be, we still must face the decisive question: Why do we even celebrate such a sacrament? Is it not mainly a relic from a distant past which has lost its discernible purpose?

The impression of irrelevance is further intensified when we remember that the main battle over the Lord's Supper concerned a word that was not even used in the original Hebrew or rather Aramaic, namely the word "is." Even going behind this word to the intention of the words of institution and deciding whether a symbolic or a real presence of Christ is intended does not alleviate one major problem. Contrary to what the potentially misleading word

"Eucharist" (i.e., thanksgiving) might convey, the Lord's Supper is not a human enterprise through which we give thanks to God and Christ for all he has done, is doing, and will do. Though this aspect should not be excluded, the Lord's Supper is primarily Christ's own doing, it is the Lord's Supper through which he mediates himself to us.

Contemporary exegesis has shown that the Lord's Supper is intimately connected with the meals that Jesus shared daily with his disciples and the meals he had with sinners and outcasts of society. Still today he invites us (sinners) to gather around his table and have table fellowship with him. That such meals do not deteriorate into mere memorial meals presupposes one essential item: The Jesus who once gathered people around him is the one who is present today too, he is the resurrected and exalted Christ. This meal is Christ's meal since he takes the initiative to invite us and is present as the host and in the elements. Any memorial aspect must always be relegated to secondary significance.

When one receives him and his meal, it is visibly demonstrated that God in Christ is no longer a distant and alienated God. He is present in and with the individual person. Thus estrangement from God has no room in the Lord's Supper and forgiveness of sins and communion with God become visible. Yet the Lord's Supper is not a sacrament of individual piety. While a specifying of the individual Christian takes place in which he or she is singled out by having communion with Christ, the presence of the gathered people points to another direction. The Lord's Supper is first and foremost an *ecclesiological* sacrament.

Through the Lord's Supper the faithful are invited to celebrate their communion with their crucified and resurrected Lord. This union should radiate through the individual members to all other members, creating and strengthening the bond of unity among all the faithful. Even beyond the individual community celebrating the Lord's Supper, this rite should express and be the symbol of the already existing unity of the whole church as Christ's body.

Altar and pulpit fellowship, proclaiming and celebrating the same mighty deeds of the one God, signify ultimate union among Christians. But the Lord's Supper is not simply a confirmation of our unity in Christ. The Lord's Supper is not our doing but Christ's. He is the main agent and the gift; and consequently we should also expect something from it, namely that the sacramental participation in Christ's body forms us into the body of Christ. Wolfhart Pannenberg comments very appropriately: the Lord's Supper is "the source and the root from which the unity of the Christians lives and is continuously renewed. This corresponds with the idea that fellowship in the Lord's Supper need not stand at the end of the process of church union, but it can also already be the present power of Christ, on the way towards this goal."[87] It is as wrong to expect that communion fellowship would magically or automatically create church union as to assume that this fellowship is only permissible if this union has already been achieved. The Lord's Supper is not only expressive of the union already existing, since Christ is present in it, but it has unifying character and can properly be celebrated together on the way toward union.

Here we should also remember that Jesus did not only have meal communion with "saints." He deliberately invited those who were on the outside, on the fringes. Thus to presuppose that first there should be union, including mutual recognition of the ministerial office, before there can be the sharing in Christ's meal runs contrary to what Christ has instituted. He is the giver and we receive as we believe. To safeguard admission to the Lord's Supper by excluding all "unworthy" people leads to the false impression that only worthy ones can receive him. Yet Jesus himself pointed out that he has come to the sinners, to those who have gone astray while the righteous do not seem to need him. If we exclude each other from the Lord's Supper we attempt to turn this meal into our own supper and actually exclude Christ himself. Christ's presence should humble us and make us aware that we are all unworthy and in need of his presence to attain the full measure of his grace.

It is significant that we read in the statement of the joint Lutheran/Roman Catholic Commission, *Ways toward Unity* (*Wege zur Einheit*), that Christ nourishes the church with his body and blood.[88] Thus not only the individual Christian is helped but the church itself is being built. As the faithful receive the body of Christ, they become one body. It is recognized here that Christ himself is the agent who gathers and assembles the faithful around his table. Christ does not divide his body but we do so by our injunctions. Restoration of unity therefore presupposes that we allow Christ to make us experience anew the unity in which we share. Paul expressed this insight well saying: "Because there is one bread, we who are many are one body, for we all partake of the one bread" (1 Cor. 10:17).

Next to the ecclesiological aspect of the Lord's Supper, but theologically speaking its actual presupposition, is the *christological aspect*. This is where the accounts of Jesus' last supper gain special significance. The decisive gift of the Lord's Supper is Christ himself with all he has wrought for us. This is the main reason why the church fought so hard to assert that Christ is really present in this meal. Mere symbolism or memory does not suffice. Certainly, the sacrament of Christ's body and blood reminds us and God of Christ's sacrifice on the cross on Good Friday. Yet his presence in the elements is decisive. Through it he sanctifies those who partake of the sacrament. If, contrary to the words of the institution, Christ is not really present in the elements, then nothing happens from Christ's side. The Lord's Supper is only our own meal at which he presides like at any other meal over which we ask his blessing. But we obtain only what we bring to it. Yet if he is really present, if his sacrifice on the cross is appropriated to us in our consuming the elements, we obtain something that we are never able to give—a renewed relationship with God, forgiveness of sins, and the prospect of eternal life.

Christ is not present as the dead Jesus on the cross. He is the living and resurrected Christ who has overcome death through his resurrection. While his sacrifice on the cross is visibly presented in the elements in a symbolic realism as the words of institution say, he beckons us to look beyond the present, where his sacrifice is appropriated to us through forgiveness and renewal, to the future, where this sacrifice will find its completion in a new life.

Since God in Christ accepts the elements of his own creation, bread and wine, we are reminded that there is no separation between the salvation provided through his body and blood and the elements of the earth. The earth is God's and participates in his redemption. Christ takes and uses the elements and identifies himself with them. This is not only a claiming of possession but a reminder that the earth is the Lord's and all within it. Salvation has a cosmic referent and is not just an interior, psychological process.

Christ's presence under bread and wine represents or rather reenacts two things: the singular sacrifice on the cross and the singular last supper that he celebrated with his disciples. The representation of the sacrifice on the cross should stimulate us to sacrifice ourselves to God, to rededicate our lives totally to him along with all that is important in our lives, our time, our possessions, and our priorities. Thus the Lord's Supper is not only celebration of Christ's past and present deeds but rededication. Similarly, the representation of the last supper should stimulate us to gather all of God's children in similar manner as he gathered his disciples, and the sinners and outcasts of society. We should form a community that shares with each other what is vital to our lives. Thus the meal community should become a community of mutual concern and of looking after one another. It should be self-evident that this has immense practical and pastoral implications. Sharing in the Lord's Supper can never remain a closed act. It energizes to open the doors for proclaiming Christ to the end of the world, to gather those on the highways and byways, and to share the food with those who like us must be fed with the bread of eternal life.

Since Christ's Spirit is called upon (the *epiklesis*) in the Supper we are sanctified and renewed through his Spirit. Such efficacy is not limited to psychological or group-dynamic results, or to a biological process, but it is truly metaphysical, opening new life. Yet as Christ shared with us, so we will also want to share this new life with others in obedient stewardship and by daily living out his will.

As the third aspect of the Eucharist we must mention the *eschatological aspect*. This has been most sorely neglected since the patristic age. When theologians of the early church talked about the Eucharist as "a medicine toward immortality" they did not mean, although it was often assumed, an increase in personal sanctification. It rather meant that the Lord present in his Supper will guide us on toward the goal of his sacrifice, to allow for us undiminished union with God. The frequent image of a celestial banquet is not unrelated to the Lord's Supper. We are celebrating with him and in his memory until he comes. It is a meal of praise and hope, of victory in principle but not yet in completion. This shows through in the translation of the early church's "Maranatha!" as an expectant shout, "Our Lord, come!" or "Come, Lord Jesus" (1 Cor. 16:22 and Rev. 22:20). The Lord's Supper is and should properly bear a festive note of celebration. Looking back to Jesus' death and resurrection, we celebrate his victory over death, and we rejoice in his living presence while gathering with him around his table. Since Christ is neither on the cross nor in the tomb, we can be assured that his victory is already won.

But the vision of the fulfillment of God's reign in the eschaton will remind any enthusiasts that his kingdom is still to come. It cannot be identified with a particular ecclesial structure or with a certain restructuring of society. Christ's veiled presence in his Supper still needs to be changed one day to the unveiled presence of the returning Lord. When we celebrate Christ's sacrifice we also remind God that this sacrifice should not be in vain, that the Parousia should not be outstanding indefinitely. The Lord's Supper is a reminder to God and us that the celestial banquet is celebrated only in anticipation but not in fullness. The eschatological aspect will prevent us from turning the Lord's Supper into a memorial meal. Our eyes are not just turned to the past, but they go forward to the future. Similar to the early Christian community, the Lord's Supper is for us a reminder that the future is still to come. But the Supper serves at the same time as a down payment that it will not remain future forever. One day God will redeem his promises.

In a twofold way the vision of the eschatological fulfillment will also help us to overcome our resignation over the supposed stagnation of the approaching kingdom and over the futility of our own efforts to bring about the kingdom. (1) Since we are looking forward to the final completion of God's reign through the Parousia of Christ, we are relieved of the awesome burden to make ourselves into the body of Christ without spot and wrinkle. We are free to admit brokenness, disunity, and failure knowing that Christ will take up all our halfhearted and awkward efforts in his new creation. (2) Yet the prospect of the eschatological fulfillment, that God will one day dwell among his people, a prospect which we celebrate in the Lord's Supper, will not render us useless or even complacent. The eschatological goal will inspire us ecclesiastically to show forth the unity that we share. It will incite us ecologically to demonstrate that God has accepted all his creation and will one day redeem it. And it will prod us socially to indicate that the solidarity around the table needs to extend beyond the Lord's Table to include every home and nation.

It is naive to assume that sharing the Lord's Supper consists just of eating a small wafer and sipping a few drops of wine or of grape juice. It is also naive to suggest that the Lord's Supper is just a memorial of Christ's death or a symbolic demonstration of the love we share. The Lord's Supper with all its facets (liturgy, actions, symbols, etc.) is the visible presence of divine grace and therefore the lifeblood of the Christian faith. It has individual and cosmic dimensions, it has ecclesial and social implications, and it touches the life of individuals and of the church as a whole. Pierre Teilhard de Chardin, perhaps, summed up best these diverse yet central dimensions of the Lord's Supper when he wrote in almost ecstatic vision in *The Divine Milieu*:

> I am beginning to understand: under the sacramental Species it is primarily through the "accidents" of matter that you touch me. . . . The arms and the heart of which you open to me are nothing less than all the united powers of the world which, penetrated and permeated to their depths by your will, . . . converge upon my being to form it, nourish it and bear it along towards the centre of your fire. . . . To the total offer that is made me, I can only answer by a total acceptance. I shall therefore *react* to the eucharistic contact with *the entire effort of my life*. . . . The Eucharist must invade my life. My life must become, as a result of the sacrament, an unlimited and endless contact with you—that life which seemed, a few moments ago, like a baptism with you in the waters of the world, now reveals itself to me as a communion with you through the world. It is the sacrament of life. *The sacrament of my life*—of my life received, of my life lived, of my life surrendered. . . .[89]

APPENDIX: THE ORDINATION TO MINISTRY

At first glance it may appear strange for a Lutheran to consider ordination to ministry within the context of word and sacraments. After all, Lutherans insist on the priesthood of all believers.[90]

Nevertheless we read in the Augsburg Confession "that nobody should publicly teach or preach or administer the sacraments in the church without regular call" (CA 14). In the third edition of his *Loci Communes* Melanchthon even pondered whether he should include ordination among the sacraments, that is, ordination as the call to serve the gospel and the public recognition of that call.[91] Though Melanchthon's desire to have ordination included among the sacraments was never acceded in Lutheran circles, it was always clear for Lutherans that the public ministerial office is never merely a delegated one. While the public office occurs in the midst of a congregation and is administered in conjunction with all the faithful, it also stands over against the congregation in its leading and guiding function.

The public office is not something one assumes but something one is called to. This call, however, though mediated through other people, is never just the call of those people. It is God's call to spread his word, a call that is subsequently verified through public calling to this office. This does not invalidate or diminish the priesthood of all believers. On the contrary, it guides and supports it.

A twofold approach to ministry—priesthood of all believers and special offices—can already be traced in the New Testament. Paul asserts that through Christ God "reconciled us to himself and gave us the ministry of reconciliation" (2 Cor. 5:18). But Paul does not assume that this ministry is automatically shared by everybody. As we see in his own case, he values very highly the office of apostle (Rom. 1:1–5); and we also hear of prophets, teachers, and evangelists (Eph. 4:11). Though the body of Christ is not fragmented, not all have the same function and the same gifts. But all of us are summoned to "declare the wonderful deeds of him who called you out of darkness into his marvelous light" (1 Peter 2:9).

At the command of the risen Lord the apostles were sent into the world to proclaim the gospel. Their special call and mission was singular and cannot be conferred upon others. Yet the postapostolic church treasured its apostolic roots. The doctrine of apostolic succession that gradually emerged in the first centuries witnesses to the normative character of its apostolic origin and reminds us that the call to mission must be continued.

The various offices of apostle, evangelist, prophet, and teacher were gradually fused into the office of bishop in the emerging church. Though there are traces of this office in the New Testament (1 Tim. 3:1; 4:14), this one comprehensive office does not stand in rectilinear continuity with the New Testament structure of the church and its offices. Yet there are some logical justifications for establishing such an office. For the sake of unity the rapidly growing church needed a reduction of "authorities" and rightly moved toward centralization of these authorities. We witness this move in the earliest synods and councils, although the church was not always successful in this attempt, as the emergence of dissenting Christian bodies shows (e.g., Monophysites, Nestorians, etc.). On an individual level, the bishop or pastor symbolizes this unity today by publicly proclaiming the Christian message and presiding over the eucharistic celebration. Despite the danger of misuse of the one office, the priestly office does not inhibit missionary activities, but should enable individual Christians to carry on this missionary endeavor. As history has shown, the gospel has often been effectively handed on through individual witness of lay people.

The Lutheran insistence that public proclaiming should not be performed "without regular call" does not preclude the teaching at home or the spreading of the gospel to one's neighbor. It states, however, that one should not assume a public teaching function without a regular call. Even in the American Sunday school system, in which presumably just about anyone is able to teach, we usually find a Sunday school superintendent or a minister of Christian education who supervises the teaching and assures that the teaching is done properly and by specially chosen teachers. The "properly called" does not refer just to the ordained priesthood. For instance, Luther mentioned more than once how important his call to the doctorate was in the face of all temptations.

While all these different aspects of the office participate in the ministry of reconciliation, the Augsburg Confession emphasizes two aspects especially well when it says: "To obtain such faith [in justification] God instituted the office of the ministry, that is, provided the Gospel and the sacraments" (CA 5). The office of ministry is concerned in a special way with the proclamation of the gospel and the administration of the sacraments. Two dangers must be avoided here. On the one hand, the teaching and sacerdotal offices dare not become so overpowering that the faithful members excuse themselves completely from active and meaningful participation in the ministry of reconciliation. This is often the danger in a clergy-dominated church. On the other hand, the proclamation of the word and the administration of the sacraments dare not become equally everybody's concern so that the diversity of the body of Christ becomes homogenized and its cohesion is attenuated through lack of clearly discernible leadership. If the unifying symbol of the teaching and sacerdotal office is unduly diminished, often individualistic sectarianism evolves in which everyone strives to obtain salvation according to his or her predilection.

The call to the ministerial office is always mediated, extended on behalf of the Lord of the church, and actualized through representatives of the institutional church. The subjective moment, when one feels called by God, always needs the outward manifestation of being called by the church. The connection with the visible church assures that we conduct our ministry in the context of the church and its living tradition, especially if we attempt to reform its present structure. The church and its ministry are never static or eternally given, as the idea of apostolic succession might wrongly suggest; they must be continuously recovered and sharpened. The Reformation insight that the church is always to be reformed also pertains to the ministry including its Protestant manifestation.

The issue of apostolic succession has often caused division within Christendom.[92] The Roman Catholic and Anglican traditions have customarily emphasized the necessity of a historical succession, depicting an unbroken line of tradition. Yet today more emphasis is placed on a material succession in the sense of the catholicity and truthfulness of the church. Most Protestant denominations would agree with the necessity of this interpretation of succession. Even the status of ordination has lost its sharply divisive nature. Common to all traditions is the public act of ordination. It is always performed in front of and with participation of the assembled congregation. Though ordination is not an act of the assembled congregation, often the congregation acknowledges that a candidate for ordination is worthy and prepared to be designated to this specific office. The candidate is also instructed in the duties of his office and promises with the help of God to fulfill them. Ordained leaders lay their hands on the candidate; they implore the assistance of the Holy Spirit for this act of ordination and for the candidate in performing his or her duties; through a liturgical act in which Scripture readings and prayers assume an important place, the candidate is inducted into the office which allows him or her to obtain the juridical and spiritual power connected with it and to perform the appropriate rites and duties. In the Protestant tradition the office is usually that of the minister, while in the Catholic tradition there exist several hierarchical levels of that office such as subdeacon, deacon, priest, etc. Yet in the full sense the office there too is that of the priest (minister).

At the Council of Trent the Roman Catholic Church spoke of ordination as conferring a spiritual and indelible character that pertains to this life, and it affirmed that ordination must be regarded as a sacrament. This twofold emphasis, indelible character and sacrament, has tended to set apart a priest from the rest of the faithful. The Council of Trent also saw the priestly function primarily in the administration of the sacraments. Vatican II then brought a more balanced view. It emphasized that though the ordained is set apart from the laity, he is not separated from them. "For priests are brothers among brothers with all those who have been reborn at the baptismal font."[93] Of course, ordination is still considered definitive. But there is nothing that hinders the church from freeing a priest temporarily or permanently from his obligation in order to return him to the condition and life of the laity. The indelible character is primarily intended to mean that one is always a priest whether "on duty" or not. Yet it is not a strictly ontological character that is conveyed at ordination. It is rather a functional disposition. The duties of a priest are now considered on much broader terms than just administration of the sacraments. The main tasks of the priest are proclamation of the word, administration of the sacraments, and performing the role of the unifying servant both within a given congregation and between congregations. With the first two items the concern of the Reformation for proclamation of the word and administration of the sacraments has been picked up. The role of unifying servant, however, is often not perceived clearly enough in the churches of the Reformation. But such a unifying factor should naturally result if we follow Paul's image of the church as the body of Christ, with the priest assuming the role of one providing integrating leadership.

The functional aspect of ordination is most strongly expressed in the Reformed tradition in which ordination primarily designates someone to the role of pastor. The Anglican tradition perceives the functional role differently by emphasis on apostolic succession. Ordination by someone standing in apostolic succession seems to assure right exercise of the office. Today, as we have seen, the emphasis is more on material succession, faithfulness in doctrine, than on formal succession. Yet in all traditions ordination is a singular act, different from installing someone to work in a particular location. Ordination, though it may be permanently or temporarily revoked, is not repeated.

In the Roman Catholic tradition since Vatican II and in the Lutheran tradition there is a certain tension in their own understandings of ordination. On the one hand, they emphasize the priesthood of all believers, indicating that all share in the office. On the other hand, they insist that a special blessing, the gift of the Holy Spirit, is imparted on the one who is ordained. Since both traditions require adequate preparation for ordination on spiritual, intellectual, and practical levels, they do not consider this rite an automatic qualification ritual that would guarantee proper fulfillment of the function of the office. Both also agree that one has already received the Holy Spirit through baptism. Thus it is highly unlikely that the one to be ordained would receive the Spirit again (twice) in contrast to other Christians. Since ordination leads to public proclamation of the word and administration of the sacraments, however, it is only proper to call upon the Spirit that the person being ordained may be properly guided and directed in the exercise of the pastoral office.

Should ordination then be considered a sacrament? Its nonrepetitive character seems to enhance its sacramental status, since it seems to confer a singular promise and obligation. There is no doubt that ordination is a solemn and sacred rite; it is not performed casually or routinely. But it cannot be derived from an express command of the resurrected Christ or a practice of Jesus of Nazareth. Admittedly, Jesus called disciples or apostles. This means that the community around Jesus and the Christian community at Pentecost were never without leaders and officers. But the office of an apostle or a prophet or an evangelist differs considerably from what we today call the priestly or pastoral office. Like any other ritual in the church, ordination is an act conducted on behalf of Christ. Yet no one is ordained because Christ said that there should be ordained ministers or priests. Ordination occurs because the resurrected Christ told his disciples: "Go therefore and make disciples of all nations" (Matt. 28:19). In carrying on as heirs of the disciples in the ministry of reconciliation, the church decided that an ordained clergy would facilitate this mission. Thus the ministry of reconciliation given by the Lord to his apostles and his command to spread the gospel are the deepest reasons for ordination. While Lutherans are not, in principle, opposed to according sacramental status to ordination, they also see no need to do so.

The controversy over the ordination of women must be seen in this light. If the ministry of reconciliation also extends to women and if the command to spread the gospel also includes women, and if such priestly office conferred upon women does not hinder or slow down the spreading of the gospel and the recognition of Christian unity, it is certainly in accordance with the will of the Lord to ordain women. The Lord reminded his disciples: "The harvest is plentiful, but the laborers are few; pray therefore the Lord of the harvest to send out laborers into his harvest" (Matt. 9:37–38). If these laborers come and are qualified, we would do the Lord a disservice by refusing to accept them. Instead we should praise the Lord that his work continues through all of us, his unworthy instruments, whom he has called to faithfulness.

NOTES

1. So rightly Friedrich Lang, "Abendmahl und Bundesgedanke im Neuen Testament," *Evangelische Theologie* 25 (1975): 524, gives us a very detailed and reliable account of the present discussion.

2. Cf. for the following the extensive treatment by Joachim Jeremias,

The Eucharistic Words of Jesus, trans. N. Perrin (rev. ed.; Philadelphia: Fortress Press, 1977), 138–203.

3. For the following, see Lang, "Abendmahl und Bundesgedanke," 529.

4. Ethelbert Stauffer, *Jesus and His Story*, trans. Richard Winston and Clara Winston (New York: Alfred A. Knopf, 1960), 113–114, mentions this possibility.

5. So rightly "Abendmahl und Bundesgedanke," 530. For a different view, cf. Rudolf Pesch, *Das Abendmahl und Jesu Todesverständnis* (Freiburg: Herder, 1978), 90, who claims that the question whether Jesus' last supper was a Passover meal is by no means a secondary issue. Yet contrary to Pesch's insistence the evidence is not that clear. Moreover, the conclusions drawn from the last supper, regardless whether it was a Passover meal, need not be that different. Cf. also Rudolf Pesch, *Wie Jesus das Abendmahl hielt. Der Grund der Eucharistie* (Freiburg: Herder, 1977). To the discussion with Pesch, cf. Eugen Ruckstuhl, "Neue und alte Überlegungen zu den Abendmahlsworten Jesu," *Studien zum Neuen Testament und seiner Umwelt*, series A, 5:79–106.

6. So Ferdinand Hahn, "Zum Stand der Erforschung der urchristlichen Hermeneutik," *Evangelische Theologie* 25 (1975): 563, who may somewhat overstate his case.

7. For the following, cf. Bernhard Lohse, "Quartodezimaner," in *RGG*[3], 5:733, and *Epistula Apostolorum* (15–26), trans. H. Duensing in E. Hennecke–W. Schneemelcher, *New Testament Apocrypha*, trans. R. McL. Wilson (London: Lutterworth Press, 1963), 1:199–209.

8. So Hahn, "Zum Stand der Erforschung," 554–55.

9. For the following, cf. Helmut Feld, *Das Verständnis des Abendmahls* (Darmstadt: Wissenschaftliche Buchgesellschaft, 1976), 77.

10. So quite correctly G. W. H. Lampe, in his noteworthy essay, "The Eucharist in the Thought of the Early Church," in *Eucharistic Theology Then and Now*, ed. R. E. Clements et al. (London: SPCK, 1968), 37.

11. Cyprian *Epistles* (63.4), in ANF 5:359.

12. Justin Martyr *Dialogue with Trypho* (41), in ANF 1:215.

13. Cf. Georg Kretschmar, "Abendmahl III/1," in *TRE* 1:63.

14. Justin Martyr *The First Apology* (66), in ANF 1:185. For the discussion of this passage, cf. Kretschmar, "Abendmahl," 67, and ANF 1:185 n. 6.

15. Irenaeus *Against Heresies* (5.2.2), in ANF 1:528.

16. For the following, cf. the perceptive comments by Kretschmar, "Abendmahl," 69.

17. Tertullian *On the Resurrection of the Flesh* (8), in ANF 1:551.

18. Irenaeus *Against Heresies* (4.18.4), in ANF 1:484.

19. Gregory of Nyssa *The Great Catechism* (37), in NPNF, second series 5:506.

20. John of Damascus *Exposition of the Orthodox Faith* (4.16), in NPNF, second series 9:88.

21. Ibid. (4.11), in NPNF 9:80.

22. Cf. Chrysostom *Baptismal Instructions* (3.23), in ACW 31:63–64, where he admonishes his listeners not to become lax since there is no second remission through baptism, but only a long and painful process of repentance.

23. For this and the following two quotes, see John of Damascus *Exposition of the Orthodox Faith* (4.13), in NPNF 9:83.

24. For this and the following two quotes, see ibid.

25. Ambrose *On the Mysteries* (9.50), in NPNF, second series 10:324.

26. Ibid. (9.58), in NPNF 10:325.

27. Cf. the article, "Grace, Means of," in *Lutheran Cyclopedia*, ed. Erwin L. Lueker (rev. ed.; St. Louis: Concordia, 1975), 345.

28. Augustine *On the Gospel of John* (26.13), in NPNF 7:172, in his exegesis of John 6:41–59.

29. Ibid. (26.19), in NPNF 7:173.

30. Augustine *Letters* (187.41), in FC 30:255.

31. Augustine *Reply to Faustus the Manichaean* (20.18), in NPNF 4:261.

32. For this quote and the next, see Gregory the Great *Dialogues* (4.60 and 4.57), in FC 39:273 and 266.

33. As quoted by Jaroslav Pelikan, *The Christian Tradition. A History of the Development of Doctrine*, vol. 3: *The Growth of Medieval Theology (600–1300)* (Chicago and London: University of Chicago Press, 1978), 79.

34. According to an opponent as quoted in ibid., 3:186.

35. Also quoted ibid., 3:187.

36. According to ibid., 3:192.

37. For a sample of these legends, see A. J. Macdonald, *Berengar and the Reform of the Sacramental System* (Merrick, N.Y.: Richwood, 1977 [1930]), 250ff.

38. So Pelikan, *Christian Tradition* 3:198–99.

39. According to Macdonald, *Berengar*, 258.

40. "The Trinity, Sacraments, Canonical Mission" (430), in Heinrich Denzinger, *The Sources of Catholic Dogma*, trans. R. J. Deferrari (St. Louis: B. Herder, 1957), 169.

41. P. Browe, *Die häufige Kommunion im Mittelalter* (Münster, 1938), 162 and 145–46, as quoted in *The Eucharist*, ed. the Lutheran/Roman Catholic Joint Commission (Geneva: Lutheran World Federation, 1980), 85.

42. Cf. for the following points, *Conrad Grebel's Programmatic Letters of 1524*, trans. J. C. Wenger (Scottdale, Pa.: Herald Press, 1970), 21–22.

43. *The Legacy of Michael Sattler*, trans. and ed. John H. Yoder (Scottdale, Pa.: Herald Press, 1973), 37.

44. For this and the following quotes, see Ulrich Zwingli, "Aus der Auslegung der 18. Schlussrede," in *Der Glaube der Reformatoren*, ed. Franz Lau (Bremen: Carl Schünemann, 1964), 292–93 (own trans.).

45. *CR* 95:86, 5–9 (own trans.).

46. Wilhelm Neuser in *Handbuch der Dogmen- und Theologiegeschichte*, vol. 2: *Die Lehrentwicklung im Rahmen der Konfessionalität*, ed. Carl Andresen (Göttingen: Vandenhoeck & Ruprecht, 1980), 264 and n. 219.

47. John Calvin, *Institutes of the Christian Religion*, vol. 2, ed. John T. McNeill and trans. Ford Lewis Battles (Philadelphia: Westminster Press, 1960), 2:1359–60 (IV, 17, 1).

48. Ibid., 1361–62 (IV, 17, 2).

49. Ibid., 1363 (IV, 17, 3).

50. Ibid., 1424 (IV, 17, 46).

51. Martin Luther, The Blessed Sacrament of the Holy and True Body of Christ, and the Brotherhoods (1519), *LW* 35:50–51.

52. Ibid., *LW* 35:56–57.

53. Ibid., *LW* 35:62–63.

54. Ibid., *LW* 35:59–60.

55. Cf. for the following, ibid., *LW* 35:49.

56. Cf. Martin Luther, A Treatise on the New Testament, that is, the Holy Mass (1520), *LW* 35:82.

57. Ibid., *LW* 35:84.

58. Ibid., *LW* 35:94.

59. Ibid., *LW* 35:80–81.

60. Cf. for the following and the quote Martin Luther, The Babylonian Captivity of the Church (1520), *LW* 36:27–28.

61. Ibid., *LW* 36:31.

62. Cf. ibid., *LW* 36:35ff.

63. Martin Luther, Smalcald Articles, in *BC,* 293–94.

64. This has also been pointed out by Reinhold Seeberg, *Lehrbuch der Dogmengeschichte* (Darmstadt: Wissenschaftliche Buchgesellschaft, 1959), 4/1:406.

65. Martin Luther, The Adoration of the Sacrament of the Holy Body of Christ (1523), *LW* 36:280.

66. Martin Luther, The Babylonian Captivity of the Church, *LW* 36:19–20.

67. Martin Luther, The Sacrament of the Body and Blood of Christ—Against the Fanatics (1526), *LW* 36:342.

68. Martin Luther, Confession Concerning Christ's Supper (1528), *LW* 37:303.

69. Ulrich Zwingli, *Amica Exegesis,* in *CR* 92:587, 15–20.

70. For this and the following quote, see the text of Article 15 in *Die Bekenntnisschriften der evangelisch-lutherischen Kirche,* 3d ed. (Göttingen: Vandenhoeck & Ruprecht, 1956), 65, 15–26.

71. Philip Melanchthon, The Augsburg Confession (10), in *BC,* 34.

72. Philip Melanchthon, Apology of the Augsburg Confession (10), in *BC,* 179.

73. Martin Luther, *Glossae D. Martini Lutheri super sententias patrum de controversia coenae exhibitas ipsi a. D. Philippo Melanchthone, WA* 38, 299.

74. Philip Melanchthon, *Epist. ad Camerar* (10.01.1535), in *CR* 2:822.

75. For this and the following quote, see *Gutachten im Ansbacher Streit um leibliches Essen und Verdauen, Worms, Sept. 1555,* in *CR* 9:277ff.

76. Variata (1540), in *Die Bekenntnisschriften der evangelisch-lutherischen Kirche*, 65.

77. Friedrich Loofs, *"Abendmahl. II. Kirchenlehre,"* in *RE*[3], 1:38.

78. Heidelberg Catechism (question 76), 129. For the following quotes, see ibid., 130.

79. So rightly at the conclusion of the Roman Catholic–Lutheran Dialogue, *The Eucharist as Sacrifice* (New York: U.S.A. National Committee of the Lutheran World Federation, 1967), 196.

80. Cf. for the following, the thoughtful comments by Paul Althaus, *Die Christliche Wahrheit. Lehrbuch der Dogmatik*, 5th ed. (Gütersloh: Gerd Mohn, 1959), 582ff.

81. Martin Luther, That These Words of Christ, "This is My Body," etc. Still Stand Firm Against the Fanatics (1527), *LW* 37:100.

82. "Decree on the Most Holy Eucharist" (874), in Denzinger, *Sources of Catholic Dogma*, 266.

83. For the extent to which both traditions agree and at which points there is still disagreement, cf. the careful study, *The Eucharist*, esp. 61–89, in the supplementary studies by Harding Meyer and Vinzenz Pfnür.

84. "Decree on the Ministry and Life of Priests" (3.13), in *The Documents of Vatican II,* 560–61.

85. Augsburg Confession (24), in *BC,* 58.

86. *Evangelischer Erwachsenenkatechismus,* ed. Werner Jentsch, et al. (Gütersloh: Gerd Mohn, 1975), 539.

87. Wolfhart Pannenberg, *Ethik und Ekklesiologie. Gesammelte Aufsätze* (Göttingen: Vandenhoeck & Ruprecht, 1977), 287.

88. *Wege zur Gemeinschaft* (17), ed. Gemeinsame römisch-katholische/evangelisch-lutherische Kommission 2d ed. (Paderborn: Bonifatius, 1981), 13–14.

89. Pierre Teilhard de Chardin, *The Divine Milieu* (New York: Harper Torchbooks, 1965), 126–27.

90. For the most comprehensive treatment of ordination and office presenting and evaluating the biblical roots, the historical divergence, and the ecumenical discussion, cf. Heinz Schütte, *Amt, Ordination und Sukzession im Verständnis evangelischer und katholischer Exegeten und Dogmatiker der Gegenwart sowie in Dokumenten ökumenischer Gespräche* (Düsseldorf: Patmos-Verlag, 1974).

91. Philip Melanchthon, *Loci Communes,* in *CR* 21: 848ff.

92. For the following, cf. the careful and balanced treatment of the priestly office in *Das geistliche Amt in der Kirche*, ed. Gemeinsame römisch-katholische/evangelisch-lutherische Kommission, (Paderborn: Bonifatius, 1981), 42ff.

93. "Decree on the Ministry and Life of Priests" (2.9), in *The Documents of Vatican II,* 552.

Postscript

We have come to the end of our investigation of word and sacraments. Considering the history of interpretation, particularly the denominational and regional emphases, one may wonder exactly what this has to do with God's self-communication. Indeed some of the interpretations of divine communication appear today as oddities that fortunately are no longer taken seriously, for example the medieval custom of witnessing as many divine presences through the "change" as possible, thus running from one Mass to another while never actually participating in the divine meal.

But historical and exegetical studies have led back to a more scripturally tenable practice of sacramental use and piety. We have also noticed an astounding convergence once the layers of separate development have been cut through. Of course, in light of all the ritual connected with the sacraments and the way in which these practices are jealously guarded, one might still wonder whether these are not eminently human fabrications. Such danger surely looms large, especially if one breaks altar and pulpit fellowship with others or excludes others from fellowship.

While sacraments have become ecclesial rites, one dare not forget that they are primarily God's gift to us through which God reminds us of his gracious action toward us. If we misappropriate them, turning them into an ungracious action toward other Christians, that is, refusing altar and pulpit fellowship, we might very well call God's judgment down upon us (cf. 1 Cor. 11:29). We must always remember that sacraments are only *entrusted* to God's church; they are fundamentally God's communication of his divine grace. Thus we always must review our sacramental practice asking whether it is still congruent with his gracious word. The word is the primary element in God's self-communication. It is the judge and corrective of all its visible embodiment.

The word, however, needs a medium through which it is communicated. The sacraments are necessary elements through which the word assumes communicable form. Since God addresses the whole person with all the senses, we dare not restrict God's self-communication to a mere auditive phenomenon (preached word). Though this is still the predominate mode of communication, we realize that there is also a body language that often communicates more strongly and much more clearly.

In light of our investigation it would be wrong, however, to regard the sacraments only as God's word clothed in sign language. For this the empirical word (miracles) would suffice. The sacraments are intimately tied to a very peculiar part of God's self-disclosive history, to the word becoming flesh in Jesus of Nazareth. But again to see the sacraments only as a celebration or remembrance of God's self-communication in Jesus of Nazareth would fall short of the mark. There are no sacraments which remind us of Jesus' nativity or of the life of Jesus in general. The sacraments are not really tied to Jesus of Nazareth, but to Jesus the Christ, that is, the crucified and risen Christ. The central sacraments of the Christian tradition, baptism and Eucharist, are therefore expressive of what God has done for us through the suffering, death, and resurrection of Jesus Christ. They are expressive of the culmination of his disclosive word in the redemptive action of Jesus Christ. They point out that the salvation provided for us on the cross really pertains to us and is individually communicated to us.

It must, of course, also be asked how one should consider the other sacraments in use in the Orthodox and Roman Catholic tradition. Here we must remember that the number seven is a sacred number and a symbol of completeness. Tradition always insisted that the other sacraments do not deserve the same status as baptism and Eucharist. Some of them point to important stages in life, such as confirmation, matrimony, and extreme unction. Others are corollary to the divine self-communication, such as ordination and penance.

There is no doubt that they are significant actions. Questionable, however, is whether they are intrinsic to the divine self-communication. Thus while their importance is not to be disputed, their relation to God's self-disclosure needs further consideration within the ecumenical dialogue. We should also note that these sacraments are not missing in the Protestant tradition. In virtually all Protestant churches marriage is blessed by the church. Also the rites of confirmation and ordination are widespread. Similarly common is the rite of confession, whether corporate or individual, and subsequent absolution. Even extreme unction has its parallel in the Lutheran custom that the sick are given private communion, though quite often together with their immediate relatives. Yet none of these important actions is unanimously endowed with sacramental status.

Although God's verbal word of law and grace provides the context for his sacramental word, the sacraments form the center of God's communication to us, especially as it is directed to us in a personal way. It is not without significance that the means by which this appropriation takes place (water, wine, and bread) were the basic ingredients for supporting human life in the Near East. Thus God takes these essential items and gives them prominent significance by transforming them into cleansing from the old life and nourishment toward eternal life. In this light any neglect of the sacraments would imply a neglect of the central salvation event.

Since the Eucharist reminds us of Christ's resurrection, it is only proper to celebrate it at least every Sunday.[1] Just as baptism needs continual reappropriation, the Eucharist forms the most obvious practice of such reappropriation, celebrating Christ's death and resurrection. Similarly to God's self-disclosure in the preached word, the sacraments testify to God's initiative. God's action is prior to any human disposition and action. He opens his heart to us in Jesus Christ, opening himself to vulnerability and rejection. But not even our rejection of Jesus led him to abandon his salvational activity. He broke through the barrier of darkness and death. As with the preached word, the visible word dare not remain unheard. It invites and asks our response. Thus baptism is God's gift and human answer to this gift.[2] Baptism points toward growth in the measure of the fullness of grace. Analogously, the Eucharist invites and asks us to respond to our participation in Christ's celestial banquet with like-minded generosity toward our fellow human beings.

Since the failure of response implies judgment, even the sacraments must be seen under the aspect of law and gospel, or rather judgment and grace. While they are powerful agents of God's grace, they are not avenues of cheap grace. They are rather instruments for sharpening our conscience and deepening our Christian faith and commitment to Christ's way. Thus orthodoxy and orthopraxis are inseparable.

Finally, we must also remember that the divine communication is not simply an ongoing process but that it is basically directed toward completion and fulfillment. The eschatological moment is intrinsic to both word and sacraments. The preached word aims toward that perfect communication when "he will dwell with them, and they shall be his people, and God himself will be with them" (Rev. 21:3). Similarly, baptism directs us toward that complete death, after which there will be no sinning and no dying; the Eucharist opens the vision of the heavenly banquet when we will be with God and enjoy him forever.

Yet neither word nor sacrament provides a metaphysical escape route from earthly reality. On the contrary, the vision and prospect of the heavenly fulfillment finds its proleptic anticipation already in the here and now when we are allowed to receive direction and guidance through the preached word, when we are accepted into the community of the new covenant, his own church, and when we experience the bond of unity with Christ in our fellow Christians as we gather around his Table. God's divine communication informs us, through word and action, that in the midst of our strife-torn world a new beginning of a better world is made, a beginning whose completion will not stand out indefinitely.

NOTES

1. So also *Baptism, Eucharist and Ministry*, Faith and Order Paper No. 111 (Geneva: World Council of Churches, 1982), 16 (31).

2. Ibid., 3 (8), where it states that baptism is "both God's gift and our human response to that gift."

Selected Bibliography

THE WORD OF GOD

Auzou, Georges. *The Word of God.* Trans. Josefa Thornton. St. Louis: Herder, 1960.

Barth, Karl. *The Word of God and the Word of Man.* Trans. D. Horton. New York: Harper Torchbooks, 1957.

Cooke, Bernard. *Ministry to Word and Sacraments. History and Theology.* Philadelphia: Fortress Press, 1976.

Crowe, Frederick E. *Theology of the Christian Word: A Study in History.* New York: Paulist Press, 1978.

Ebeling, Gerhard. *God and Word.* Trans. J. W. Leitch. Philadelphia: Fortress Press, 1967.

———. *Word and Faith.* Trans. J. W. Leitch. Philadelphia: Fortress Press, 1963.

Ferré, Nels F. S. *The Universal Word: A Theology for a Universal Faith.* Philadelphia: Westminster Press, 1969.

Hamilton, Kenneth. *Words and the WORD.* Grand Rapids: Wm. B. Eerdmans, 1971.

Milner, Paulinus, ed. *The Ministry of the Word.* London: Burns & Oates, 1967.

Von Allmen, Jean-Jacques. *Preaching and Congregation.* Trans. B. L. Nicholas. London: Lutterworth Press, 1962.

Williams, R. R., ed. *Word and Sacrament.* London: SPCK, 1968.

THE SACRAMENTS

Arndt, Elmer J. F. *The Font and the Table.* London: Lutterworth Press, 1967.

Berkouwer, G. C. *The Sacraments.* Trans. Hugo Bekker. Grand Rapids: Wm. B. Eerdmans, 1969.

Clark, Neville. *An Approach to the Theology of the Sacraments.* Naperville, Ill.: Alec R. Allenson, 1956.

Davies, John G. *The Spirit, the Church and the Sacraments.* London: Lutterworth Press, 1954.

Empie, Paul C., and Austin T. Murphy, eds. *Lutherans and Catholics in Dialogue. I–III.* Minneapolis: Augsburg, 1968.

Häring, Bernard. *The Sacraments in a Secular Age.* Slough, Eng.: St. Paul Publications, 1976.

Jenson, Robert W. *Visible Words. The Interpretation and Practice of Christian Sacraments.* Philadelphia: Fortress Press, 1978.

Joyce, J. Daniel. *The Place of Sacraments in Worship.* St. Louis: Bethany Press, 1967.

Lemming, Bernard. *Principles of Sacramental Theology.* 2d ed. Westminster, Md.: Newman Press, 1960.

Baptism, Eucharist and Ministry. Faith and Order Paper No. 111. Geneva: World Council of Churches, 1982.

Rahner, Karl. *The Church and the Sacraments.* Trans. W. J. O'Hara. New York: Herder & Herder, 1963.

Schmemann, Alexander. *Sacraments and Orthodoxy.* New York: St. Vladimir's Seminary Press, 1965.

BAPTISM AND CONFIRMATION

Barth, Karl. *The Teaching of the Church Regarding Baptism.* Trans. E. A. Payne. London: SCM Press, 1948.

Beasley-Murray, George R. *Baptism in the New Testament.* New York: Macmillan Co., 1962.

Cullmann, Oscar. *Baptism in the New Testament.* Trans. J. K. S. Reid. London: SCM Press, 1950.

Dix, Gregory. *The Theology of Confirmation in Relation to Baptism.* Oxford: Basil Blackwell & Mott, 1946.

Fischer, John D. C. *Christian Initiation: Baptism in the Medieval West.* London: SPCK, 1965.

———. *Christian Initiation. Some Early Reformed Rites of Baptism and Confirmation and Other Contemporary Documents.* London: SPCK, 1970.

Kavanagh, Aidan. *The Shape of Baptism: The Rite of Christian Initiation.* New York: Pueblo Publishing, 1980.

Klos, Frank, ed. *Confirmation and First Communion.* Minneapolis: Augsburg, 1968.

Neunheuser, Burkhard. *Baptism and Confirmation.* Trans. J. J. Hughes. London: Burns & Oates, 1964.

Wagner, Günter. *Pauline Baptism and the Pagan Mysteries.* Trans. J. P. Smith. Edinburgh: Oliver & Boyd, 1967.

EUCHARIST

Brilioth, Yngve. *Eucharistic Faith and Practice. Evangelical and Catholic.* London: SPCK, 1930.

Clark, Francis. *Eucharistic Sacrifice and the Reformation.* 2d ed. London: Basil Blackwell & Mott, 1967.

Clements, Ronald E., et al. *Eucharistic Theology Then and Now.* London: SPCK, 1968.

Cochrane, Arthur C. *Eating and Drinking with Jesus. An Ethical and Biblical Inquiry.* Philadelphia: Westminster Press, 1974.

The Eucharist. Lutheran/Roman Catholic Joint Commission. Geneva: Lutheran World Federation, 1980.

George, Alfred R. *Communion with God in the New Testament.* London: Epworth Press, 1953.

Higgins, Angus J. B. *The Lord's Supper in the New Testament.* London: Regnery, 1952.

Hook, Norman. *The Eucharist in the New Testament.* London: Lutterworth Press, 1964.

Irwin, Kevin W. *American Lutherans and Roman Catholics in Dialogue on the Eucharist: A Methodological Critique and Proposal.* Rome: Editrice Anselmiana, 1979.

Jeremias, Joachim. *The Eucharistic Words of Jesus.* Trans. Norman Perrin. Rev. ed. Philadelphia: Fortress Press, 1977.

Kilmartin, Edward J. *The Eucharist in the Primitive Church.* Englewood Cliffs, N.J.: Prentice-Hall, 1965.

Marshall, I. Howard. *Last Supper and Lord's Supper.* Exeter: Paternoster Press, 1980.

Wainwright, Geoffrey. *Eucharist and Eschatology.* London: Epworth Press, 1971.

Index of Names

Index of Biblical References

Index of Subjects